Photograph by George Platt Lynes

Marianne
MOORE

a reference guide

A
Reference
Publication
in
Literature

Ronald Gottesman
Editor

Marianne MOORE

a reference guide

CRAIG S. ABBOTT

G.K.HALL&CO.
70 LINCOLN STREET, BOSTON, MASS.

Copyright © 1978 by Craig S. Abbott

Library of Congress Cataloging in Publication Data
Abbott, Craig S   1941-
   Marianne Moore, a reference guide.

   (A Reference publication in literature)
   Includes index.
   1. Moore, Marianne, 1887-1972 — Bibliography.
I. Title.   II. Series.
Z8592.65.A24   016.811'5'2   78-14318
ISBN 0-8161-8061-X

This publication is printed on permanent/durable acid-free paper
MANUFACTURED IN THE UNITED STATES OF AMERICA

Contents

Introduction

Marianne Moore has been called one of "the most interesting American poets of the day" (1921.2), the best poet except for Wallace Stevens (1922.3), "the best poet now living in America" (1925.1), a maker of "pure poetry unmatched in American literature except by Poe" (1925.19), the author of "part of the small body of durable poetry written in our time" (1935.18), "a major poet of our time" (1941.11), "our most distinguished American poet" (1944.4), "the best living American poet" (1951.1), "an imperceptible vitamin of little-known properties whose absence could prove terminal" (1965.7), "the greatest living poet in English" (1966.4), and "the best woman poet in English" (1967.19).

But, as others have noted, she has been more acclaimed than discussed. Surprisingly little has been written about this poet who was a major figure in the New Poetry movement of the early twentieth century and who continued to write into the 1970s. There is no biography, no collections of her letters, and no satisfactory edition of her works. As of 1976, only three book-length studies of her work have been published. There has been one article in the journal PMLA and none in American Literature.

The lack of a biography may soon be corrected by Clive E. Driver, Moore's literary executor and director of the Rosenbach Foundation. Until then, it is possible to piece together the facts of Moore's life from interviews (especially 1961.8, 1965.11), a New Yorker profile (1957.27), obituaries (especially 1972.20), entries in biographical dictionaries (e.g., 1942.1, 1955.3, 1970.8), and other sources. It may turn out that the biography will be, as Moore warned Bernard Engel, a "very tame affair" (1964.9). In outline it seems so. Moore was born 15 November 1887 in Kirkwood, near St. Louis, Missouri, to Mary Warner and John Milton Moore. She never saw her father, who suffered a mental breakdown before she was born. At Bryn Mawr College she found more interest—or at least encouragement—in biology than in English, though she did write for the undergraduate literary magazine Tipyn O'Bob. After receiving a B.A. in 1909, she attended Carlisle Commercial College, spent a summer in France and England, taught commercial subjects at the U.S. Indian School in Carlisle (1911-1915).

Introduction

With her mother, who continued to live with her until her death in
1947, she moved to Chatham, New Jersey, in 1916 and then, two years
later, into the literary scene in Greenwich Village, where Moore
taught in a private school and later worked in a branch of the New
York Public Library. In 1915 her poems had appeared in the Egoist,
Poetry, and Others. Without Moore's knowledge, Hilda Doolittle and
Winifred Bryher saw to the publication of Poems by the Egoist Press
in 1921. It was followed in 1924 by Observations and in later years
by some eighteen other major volumes of poetry, prose, and translations. In 1925 she became acting editor, then editor, of the Dial,
one of the most influential literary magazines of the time. In 1929
the Dial ceased publication, and Moore and her mother moved to Brooklyn, at least in part to be nearer Moore's brother, John Warner Moore,
then a chaplain assigned to the Brooklyn Navy Yard. She remained in
Brooklyn, writing, translating, and winning acclaim, until late 1965
or early 1966, when she moved to Manhattan. She died there 5 February
1972. Her papers, even her re-created living room, are at the Rosenbach Foundation in Philadelphia. They include her library, manuscripts,
diaries from 1919 to 1969, about 35,000 pieces of correspondence, and
other items. The Marianne Moore Newsletter, the first issue of which
appeared in spring 1977, promises to describe the collection as it is
arranged and catalogued.

The early criticism of Moore's work established terms and themes
that have echoed down to the present. Even before the publication of
Poems in 1921, Moore was being labeled "fastidious" (1918.2) and "eccentric" (1919.1), and her supposed obscurity and emotional restraint
were the subject of discussion (1916.1, 1918.1, 1918.3, 1919.1). Critics were not sure what to make of Moore's poetry. They called it a
product of wit (1921.3) and both attacked (1921.1) and praised (1921.4)
its use of prose rhythms. (These early critics seem not to have discovered the syllabic basis of Moore's stanzas.) The chief question,
the focus of a "symposium" on Moore in Poetry (1922.3), was whether
Moore was a poet at all. The later acclaim that Moore received should
not obscure the fact that there were strong objections to her work.
Three influential figures of the time denied that it was poetry. Louis
Untermeyer attacked her in his review of Others 1916. Commenting on
her exclusion from "most anthologies of American poetry," he called
her creations "highly intellectualized dissertations" (1919.1). (By
"most anthologies" he meant his own Modern American Poetry, which did
not include Moore until the third revised edition in 1925, even then
calling her the author of "criticism" rather than poetry.) Later he
came to praise Moore, faintly, but in doing so also quoted his earlier
estimate of her work as witty geometry. His view, and some of his
language, was shared by Harriet Monroe, editor of Poetry, who was not
comfortable with wit and intellect at the expense of feeling. Although
Poetry printed five of Moore's poems in its May 1915 issue, no more
appeared until June 1932. Margaret Anderson's Little Review printed
but one of Moore's poems. In her Little Review Anthology, Anderson
admitted that she did not consider Moore a poet (1953.1). Among the
earliest favorable critics of Moore's poetry were Ezra Pound,

T. S. Eliot, Hilda Doolittle, William Carlos Williams, and E. E. Cummings. Unlike Untermeyer, Monroe, and Anderson, these poets viewed Moore's poems--"delicate mechanisms," as Williams called them (1921.5) --with more understanding and with high praise.

The appearance of Observations in 1924 established Moore's reputation as more than a literary radical associated with Alfred Kreymborg's "Others" group. Reaction to it, though, was still divided between attacks for its being too intellectual and praise for its being precise in description and "aristocratic." The book won Moore the Dial Award, and in the issues of the Dial following the announcement of the award were a series of advertisements for Moore that culminated in the announcement that she would become editor. Work on the Dial took time from Moore's own writing of poetry. (Her brief reviews and editorial comments in the Dial have generally been overlooked.) Not until 1935 did another collection of her poetry appear. The introduction to this Selected Poems was written by Eliot, who placed Moore's poetry in "the small body of durable poetry written in our time," asserted that it worked to maintain the English language, found emotion combined with intellect, and praised the use of light rhyme as a counterpoint to meter and meaning (1935.8). Most reviewers of the volume cited or echoed Eliot's introduction, in its praise as well as its substance. Perceptive critics such as R. P. Blackmur (1935.3) and Kenneth Burke (1935.5) also began to comment on Moore's method of using the particular to discover the metaphysical. Eliot's comment in his introduction that Moore was an original, without any poetic derivations, seems to have met with general agreement, although critics have seen affinities in such authors as Bacon, Donne, Lyly, Dickinson, Wilde, Laforgue, James, Eliot, Cummings, and others.

In his discussion of Selected Poems, Blackmur provides us with an example of one of the difficulties confronting Moore's critics--the bibliographical complexity of the body of her work. Blackmur found the Selected Poems version of "Poetry" superior to the Observations version. He did not realize that there were two Observations versions and that he was discussing the thirteen-line version of the second printing, not the first-printing version that is reverted to (with slight changes) in Selected Poems. Moore not only added poems to the body of her work but frequently revised earlier work, sometimes in response to criticism. So too is the chronology of Moore's poetry confusing. Sandra Hochman, reviewing Tell Me, Tell Me, claimed that "Sun," the last poem in the book, was "intricate and amazingly unlike her previous work" (1967.20). But "Sun" was previous work, having first appeared in Contemporary Verse in 1916 (in a somewhat different version, of course).

After Observations, Moore published What Are Years (1941) and Nevertheless (1944). These slim volumes--fifteen poems in the first, six in the second--were seen as warmer, less remote than her earlier work. "In Distrust of Merits," a war poem, was uncharacteristically impassioned. Nonetheless, Moore was also seen to be persevering in her old style and method, which some continued to find freakish and others technically brilliant. By 1945, Randall Jarrell could complain that Moore was already seen "less as a poet than as an institution." With the exception of essays by Jarrell (1942.4, 1945.9), Burke (1942.2), Winters (1937.3), Zabel (1936.5), the Times Literary Supplement (1936.1), and Blackmur (1935.3), there was little perceptive, detailed criticism of her work. The publication of a Marianne Moore issue of the Quarterly Review of Literature in 1948 added a few good essays, namely those by Brooks (1948.4), Frankenberg (1948.7), and Koch (1948.8), all of which explore the relationship between image and idea in Moore's poetry.

Throughout these years, Moore's public remained small but was growing. The American edition of Selected Poems sold only 864 copies from its publication on 11 April 1935 to the final accounting in 1942. What Are Years sold 1,251 copies between 1941 and 1948. Nevertheless went through three printings totaling over 4,000 copies. Collected Poems appeared in 1951 and sold 6,647 copies (in the American edition) in the first year. Its sales and Moore's reputation were aided, of course, by its winning for her the National Book Award, Bollingen Prize, and Pulitzer Prize.

Reviewers of Collected Poems both complained about the narrow range of Moore's subject matter and began giving more notice to the ethical or moral basis of her art--a basis that many earlier critics, caught up in the oddities of Moore's syllabic verse, use of quotations, and style, had neglected. With increased acclaim also came more interest in Moore as a public figure. She became a celebrity. Her interest in baseball, which Kreymborg had described years before in his autobiography (1925.8), became the delight of some and the embarrassment of others. Her ode to the Dodgers, "Hometown Piece for Messrs. Alston and Reese," appeared on the front page of the New York Herald Tribune (3 October 1956), and in 1968 she threw out the first ball on opening day at Yankee Stadium. She took tours of zoos (1953.3), modeled hats, was selected as one of the six most successful women of the year (1953.7), was the subject of a New Yorker profile that pictured her as a complex chatterbox, and engaged in correspondence with the Ford Motor Company in an attempt to assist in finding a name for the car that turned out to be the Edsel.

At least as early as 1941, Moore had been called a fabulist (1941.6) because of her frequent use of animals and her concern with moral questions. And in 1945 she began some nine-years' work on the translation of the fables of Jean de La Fontaine. When they appeared in 1954, they were found successful by some (e.g., 1954.14, 1954.16) and "terrible" by others (1954.20, 1954.21). Predilections, a collection of her essays and reviews that appeared in the following year also had a mixed reception, one reminiscent of the early reception of her poetry. Reviewers were confused by her elliptical, impressionistic, mosaic technique. The most perceptive and favorable reactions came from some of the same critics who had best discussed her poetry (e.g., 1956.9).

Moore's later volumes of poetry--including Like a Bulwark (1956), O to Be a Dragon (1959), A Marianne Moore Reader (1961), The Arctic Ox (1964), and Tell Me, Tell Me (1966)--were greeted as the work of "a living legend," though still an eccentric one, perhaps even a bit of a Mary Poppins one. Especially the more public and occasional of the poems in these volumes were seen by critics such as Hugh Kenner as sentimental and as the result of mannerism imposed on platitude (1963.10). Although Moore's style, method, and subjects did not undergo drastic change through her career, her early critics charged her with emotional frigidity and some of her later critics with sentimentality. And while early she was seen as a literary radical, she came to be dismissed by some as a mere "academic" poet (1959.11).

Still, most of the criticism was favorable. Moreover, articles on Moore's themes and prosody began appearing in scholarly journals; the first of several doctoral dissertations was written (1956.16); the New York Public Library issued a bibliography (1958.16); she was interviewed for the Paris Review (1961.8); a festschrift, more appreciative than critical, celebrated her seventy-seventh birthday (1964.33); and the first full-length study of her work showed it to be a paradoxical union of objectivism and a desire to affirm values (1964.9). In 1967, on Moore's eightieth birthday, Viking and Macmillan jointly published her Complete Poems, which, true to pattern, was met with more adulation than discussion. Since then, much of the best criticism of Moore has been collected in one volume (1968.28) and two more full-length "introductions" to her poetry have appeared (1969.18, 1970.6).

For some, Moore has been a "crowning curio" like the "Camperdown Elm"; for others she has been "The Hero," going "where there is personal liking" and seeing "the rock / crystal thing to see." Both attitudes are represented in this reference guide. I have attempted to list and abstract, year by year from 1916 through 1976, all substantial criticism of Moore, including articles, books, and parts of books. For the light they shed on Moore's life, for their evidence as to the assimilation of Moore by American culture, and for their sometimes penetrating comments about Moore's work, I have also included a large but merely representative selection of comments, reviews, notices, and the like from the national press, little magazines, and other sources. I have seen and read almost all of the items; those not seen are marked by an asterisk and attributed to a source in another bibliography.

In preparing this guide I have had the help of Anthony S. Bliss, who translated the French articles; Gustaaf Van Cromphout, who translated the Dutch; Steve Franklin, who searched the Late City Edition of the New York Times; and Derek Furstenwerth, who assisted with the index.

Principal Works
by Marianne Moore

1921   Poems. London: Egoist Press.

1923   Marriage. Manikin Number Three. New York: Monroe Wheeler.

1924   Observations. New York: Dial Press.

1935   Selected Poems. New York: Macmillan; London: Faber & Faber.

1936   The Pangolin and Other Verse. London: Brendin.

1941   What Are Years. New York: Macmillan.

1944   Nevertheless. New York: Macmillan.

1945   Rock Crystal. Translated by Moore and Elizabeth Mayer. New York: Pantheon.

1951   Collected Poems. New York: Macmillan; London: Faber & Faber.

1954   The Fables of La Fontaine. Translated by Moore. New York: Viking.

1955   Predilections. New York: Viking; London: Faber & Faber.

1955   Selected Fables of La Fontaine. London: Faber & Faber.

1956   Like a Bulwark. New York: Viking. (London: Faber & Faber, 1957.)

1959   O to Be a Dragon. New York: Viking.

1961   A Marianne Moore Reader. New York: Viking.

1962   The Absentee. Based on a novel by Maria Edgeworth. New York: House of Books.

1963   Puss in Boots, The Sleeping Beauty & Cinderella. Translated by Moore. New York: Macmillan.

1964   The Arctic Ox. London: Faber & Faber.

1966   Tell Me, Tell Me: Granite, Steel, and Other Topics. New York:
        Viking.

1967   The Complete Poems of Marianne Moore. New York: Macmillan/
        Viking. (London: Faber & Faber, 1968.)

1969   Selected Poems. London: Faber & Faber.

Writings about Marianne Moore 1916-1976

1916

1   D[OOLITTLE], H[ILDA]. "Marianne Moore." The Egoist, 3 (August), 118-19.
    I believe that Moore's poems do have meaning; certainly they present beauty that is much needed nowadays.

1918

1   [ELIOT, T. S.] "Observations." The Egoist, 5 (May), 69-70. Signed "T. S. Apteryx."
    Of the work in Others, edited by Alfred Kreymborg, that by Moore "is particularly interesting." She is intellectual without being abstract and fuses thought and feeling more completely than Laforgue.

2   H[OYT], H[ELEN]. Review of Others (1917), edited by Alfred Kreymborg. Poetry, 11 (February), 275.
    Moore's poetry is unique and sometimes "too fastidious."

3   POUND, EZRA. "Others." The Little Review, 4 (March), 56-58.
    The Others anthology for 1917 contains "the first adequate presentation of Mina Loy and Marianne Moore." Their poetry is "distinctly American." Moore's verse, unlike Loy's, has "traces of emotion," but both poets are "followers of Jules Laforgue," writing "logopoeia"--poetry as "a dance of the intelligence among words and ideas."
    Reprinted: 1953.16, 1969.28, 1973.12.

1919

1   UNTERMEYER, LOUIS. "Others." In his The New Era in American Poetry. New York: Henry Holt and Co., pp. 312-13.
    Others 1916, an anthology of "literary extremists," is marked by "deliberate eccentricity" and "unconscious

1920

incongruity." Moore's "To Statecraft Embalmed" is typical
of the "strained vociferations" it contains.

1920

1   M[ONROE], H[ARRIET]. Review of Others for 1919, edited by
       Alfred Kreymborg. Poetry, 17 (December), 154.
          Moore is at least to be commended "for going her own way."

2   WILLIAMS, WILLIAM CARLOS. "Marianne Moore." Contact, [no. 1]
       (December), p. 4.
          Poem.

1921

1   ANON. Review of Poems. The Times Literary Supplement, no.
       1,018 (21 July), p. 471.
          Moore has not much to say. She writes "clumsy prose"
       and attempts to "attract attention" by tricks of spacing
       and printing. She does not know that in poetry there should
       be a harmony of form and expression. She disguises "lack
       of inspiration by means of a superficial unconventionality."

2   SITWELL, EDITH. "Reviews." The Sackbut, 2 (December), 38.
          Like the other verse in Poems, "Black Earth" is strange
       and interesting, "thick and uncouth," a product of life
       rather than art. Moore is "among the most interesting Amer-
       ican poets of the day." Her trick of ending a line in the
       middle of a word is irritating.

3   VAN DOREN, MARK. "Woman of Wit." The Nation, 113 (26 October),
       481-82.
          Moore, like Edna St. Vincent Millay and Anna Wickham,
       would be more at home in the seventeenth century. Theirs
       is a poetry of wit. In Poems, Moore has "wedded wit" but
       forsaken beauty and sense. Earlier, she contributed poems
       to Alfred Kreymborg's Others that made the anthology "dif-
       ficult to take seriously."

4   [WATSON, JAMES SIBLEY.] "American Letter." The Dial, 70 (May),
       562-68. Signed "W. C. Blum."
          The American public has overlooked "several first rate
       poets"--Pound, Cummings, Williams, and Moore. Moore writes
       lines that are like "classical prose"; she invents or appro-
       priates quotations; and "she uses the most matter-of-fact

constructions, critical rather than poetic phrases, so that extraordinary expansions of mood are uncovered without warning."

5   WILLIAMS, WILLIAM CARLOS. Untitled introduction to Moore's "Those Various Scalpels" and "In the Days of Prismatic Color." Contact, [no. 2] (January), p. 1.
      Some deny that intellectual works can be called poetry. But emotion is the force behind intellect; indeed, intellect is a kind of refined emotion. The "Whitman, windy-prairie tradition" should not obscure the fact that poems may also be "more delicate mechanisms." We are pleased to publish Moore.

1922

1   BARRINGTON, PAULINE. "Poems." Lyric West, 2 (September), 29-30. Moore's Poems is sometimes obscure but "always interesting." Hers is not "the saccharine stuff" one often finds today.

2   [CUMMINGS, E. E.] "Notes [on Contributors]." Secession, no. 2 (July), inside front cover.
      Endorses the "Secession campaign against Louis Untermeyer, an anthologist best known for the omission of William Carlos Williams and Marianne Moore from his Modern American Poetry."

3   M[ONROE], H[ARRIET]. "A Symposium on Marianne Moore." Poetry, 19 (January), 208-16.
      Differences of opinion about Moore's poetry raise the question of the definition of poetry. H. D. calls Moore a poet; Yvor Winters thinks her our best poet except for Wallace Stevens; Winifred Bryher calls her poems "perfect but static studies" produced by a person who has been denied experience; Marion Strobel calls them dull "contortions of Miss Moore's well-developed mind"; Pearl Andelson thinks they are hybrids of prose and poetry. Moore is a poet but is "too sternly controlled by a stiffly geometrical intellectuality." Afraid of sentimentality, she suppresses emotion and produces prose that sometimes becomes poetry. Her rhythms are discordant; her stanza forms are arbitrary; and her wit is a "grim and haughty humor."
      Excerpted: 1960.17.

1923

1   ELIOT, T. S. "Marianne Moore." The Dial, 75 (December),
       594-97.
          The work of only five contemporary poets "excites me as
       much as, or more than, Miss Moore's." The distinction be-
       tween aristocratic and proletariat art in Glenway Wescott's
       introduction to Marriage (1923.5) is misleading. Aristo-
       cratic art is a refinement, not an antithesis, of popular
       art. Moore's poetry is indeed aristocratic. Although "it
       can please a very small number of people," it draws its
       sustenance from the soil. Her poetry contains three ele-
       ments: "a quite new rhythm" produced in part by the fading
       of one image into another, the use of "the curious jargon
       produced in America by universal university education," and
       "an almost primitive simplicity of phrase." Finally, Moore's
       poetry, like Christina Rossetti's, is feminine in a way that
       is "a positive virtue."
          Reprinted: 1969.28.

2   J[OSEPHSON], M[ATTHEW]. "Poems: Marianne Moore." Broom, 4
       (January), 138-39.
          Most American women poets, including Gertrude Stein and
       Amy Lowell, are coarse and loud and lack both humility and
       originality. But in Moore, humility and knowledge combine
       to produce poetry that does not sob or throw back "the hair
       with disheveled hands" but that is marked by "great mystery
       and great tranquility." She draws conclusions from observa-
       tions and declaims in the "purest traditions of the English
       language."

3   UNTERMEYER, LOUIS. "Marianne Moore." In his American Poetry
       since 1900. New York: Henry Holt and Co., pp. 362-68.
          Reprint of 1923.4.

4   _____. "Poetry or Wit." The Freeman, 6 (7 February), 524.
          Moore has not appeared in "most anthologies of contempo-
       rary American poetry," has had to wait eight years for the
       publication of Poems, and has been little discussed by
       critics. The reason is that while she "has elected to of-
       fer her highly intellectualized dissertations in the form
       of poetry, she is not, in spite of the pattern of her lines,
       a poet." I admire her "acidulous and astringent quality."
       Her works display "a surface of flickering irony, a nimble
       sophistication beneath which glitter the depths of a cool
       and continually critical mind." But poetry must be based

in ecstasy. She produces wit, not poetry. She belongs to
a group of poets who write with "intellectual dexterity,
technical preciosity and...a tone that alternates between obscurity and condescension."
   Reprinted: 1923.3.

5   WESCOTT, GLENWAY. "Miss Moore's Observations." 4 pp. laid in
    Moore's <u>Marriage</u>. Manikin Number 3. New York: Monroe
    Wheeler.
       Contemporary criticism is coming to recognize "a schism
    in the body of art." There is on the one hand "a proletar-
    iat art" with "obvious honesty and simple destiny, realistic
    farce and instructive tragedy." And on the other is "aris-
    tocratic art, emulating the condition of ritual." Moore's
    is aristocratic. <u>Poems</u> contains delightfully difficult
    poems written more for thought than for eye or ear. The
    perceptions contained in the poems are those "where the con-
    sciousness meets with episodes or objective creatures."
    Moore's obscurity arises from the unfamiliarity of her ideas
    and emotions. She excites emotion by "conjunction" of per-
    ception and by rhythm. Missing from <u>Poems</u> are some of her
    early works, such as "Like a Bulwark," "Sojourn in the
    Whale," "French Peacock," "A Grave," "To an Intra-Mural
    Rat," and "He Made This Screen." Moore's poetry gives the
    impression of "frank brilliance" and "nobility," of "pro-
    found but not irreverent analysis." Although her language
    is often abstract, she does not generalize or argue. She
    "reanimates" words.

1924

1   ANON. "Marianne Moore Wins Dial Prize of $2,000." <u>The New
    York Times</u>, 23 December, p. 35.
       Moore, an assistant at the Hudson Park branch of the New
    York Public Library, has been awarded the Dial prize in rec-
    ognition of distinguished service to American letters. The
    award is given to young American writers whose work promises
    growth and development.

1925

1   ALDINGTON, RICHARD. Review of <u>Observations</u>. <u>The Criterion</u>, 3
    (July), 588-94.
       Moore is more subtle than Cocteau. Her poetry is built
    on observation and intellect, avoids emotion, uses unusual

1925

line patterns, and reveals irony, especially in quotations.
Moore, "the best poet now living in America," is original
without self-consciousness.

2   ANON. "Miss Marianne Moore." The Criterion, 3 (April), 343.
Moore has received the annual Dial award for literature.
Unlike most American poets of the last ten years, she has
discovered "an original rhythm."

3   ANON. "The New Euphues." The New York Times, 8 February, sec.
2, p. 6.
In its editorial on awarding its prize to Moore, the Dial
"falls into...a solemn frolic of fancy." The editorialist
seems to think that good poetry is obscure so that, lost
within it, a reader "will not only see the light, but the
chromatized enkindled driftwood burning at the junction and
conjunction." He compares Moore to Bacon, much to the dis-
advantage of Bacon. His own prose reminds one of Gongora,
Euphues, Pound, and Gertrude Stein.

4   ANON. Review of Observations. The Booklist, 22 (October), 23.
Observations is "a collection of obscure, highly artifi-
cial and technically elaborate poems" of limited appeal that
are in the school of Cummings and Pound.

5   GILMORE, LOUIS. "Observations." The Double Dealer, 7 (June),
200.
Moore's poetry is too original and "too cerebral" to ever
gain much popularity. Moore is "a poet's poet."

6   GORMAN, HERBERT S. "Miss Moore's Art Is Not a Democratic One."
The New York Times Book Review, 74 (1 February), 5.
Moore has produced less work and is lesser known than
previous recipients of the Dial award. Anyone interested
in contemporary American poetry must know "her sharp, intel-
lectually compact, aristocratic work." The poems in Observations result from Moore's "mental agility" and "detached
precision." Of the two paths in contemporary poetry--prim-
itivistic simplicity and formalized complexity--she has
chosen the latter, and her complexity of technique matches
the complexity of her observations. Thus her poetry is not
democratic. Emotion is present as "emotion of the mind."
"Those Various Scalpels" is typical of her work, with its
mathematical technique and its combination of pictures and
thoughts.

7   HUMPHRIES, ROLFE. "Precieuse, Model 1924." The Measure, no.
53 (July), pp. 15-17.

A comparison of some lines from Observations with some from Emily Dickinson reveals the similarities of the two poets, though Dickinson has more "passion for life" than Moore does.

8   KREYMBORG, ALFRED. Troubadour: An Autobiography. New York: Boni and Liveright, pp. 239, 242-45, 332-33, 336.
Moore, who talked in the same style that she wrote, was among the "Others" group that met at Kreymborg's. Her intellectuality was much admired. She even knew, from reading, about baseball. When Scofield Thayer heard Moore read "England" at a party given by Lola Ridge, he asked her to resubmit it to the Dial. She was the first of the "Others" to be accepted by the magazine.

*9 LARSSON, R. ELLSWORTH. Review of Observations. Voices, 4 (February), 121-24.
Listed in Sheehy and Lohf (1958.17), p. 33.

10 ROSENFELD, PAUL. "Marianne Moore." In his Men Seen: Twenty-Four Modern Authors. New York: The Dial Press, pp. 165-73.
Moore's verse seems at first a mere collection of "exquisite perceptions," but the perceptions fuse, partly through a "genteel evenness of tone" that does not obscure her intense feeling. Her wit is "subtle and ingenious"; her perception, keen; her expression, apt.

11 SEAVER, EDWIN. "A Literalist of the Imagination." The Nation, 120 (18 March), 297-98.
Earlier Dial awards have gone to authors of established reputation (Sherwood Anderson, T. S. Eliot, and Van Wyck Brooks). Granting the award to Moore, the editors have "taken an option on the future." Moore's Observations shows her to be a conservative modernist. Hers is "rigorous, supple, puritanical, generous mentality that is simple and sophisticated at the same time." At times she is obscure, but her poems are worth the effort.

12 SNOW, WILBERT. "A Literalist of the Imagination." The New York Herald Tribune Books, 2 (17 May), p. 3.
Although Moore is obscure and nonmusical, she is "a significant figure in modern American poetry"--in the same camp with Pound, Stevens, Cummings, and Eliot. Like Cummings, she divides words between lines. Like Eliot, she fills her poems with quotations, which (as in "England") are superior to her own words. She is better in her short pieces, which prevent the sort of straying found in "Nothing will Cure the Sick Lion but to Eat an Ape." She is more "epigrammatist"

1925

than poet. Some of her lines are "devoid of rhythm and
imaginative lift"; some contain farfetched figures. But
there is "a real poetic quality" in her concern with "the
odds and ends of life," her avoidance of "industrial ugli-
ness," and her occasional fine phrasing (as in "Talisman").
Contact with "our discouraging civilization" enforces her
snobbishness and satirical aloofness. Like others of her
group, she is fond of the esthetics of Oscar Wilde and George
Moore and is thus inferior to poets like Kipling, Masefield,
Frost, Robinson, and Millay.

13   [THAYER, SCOFIELD.] "Announcement." The Dial, 78 (January),
      89-90.
          The Dial award for this year "recognizes the unusual lit-
      erary virtue" of Moore, who is America's most distinguished
      poetess since Emily Dickinson. Though she has hitherto been
      largely unacclaimed, Eliot ranks her "among the half-dozen
      most 'exciting' contemporary European and American poets."

14   _____. "Comment." The Dial, 78 (February), 174-80. Titled
      "Marianne Moore and Sir Francis Bacon" in the semiannual
      index.
          While the sentences of both Moore and Sir Francis Bacon
      achieve that compression which is "the first grace of style,"
      Moore's also rise to poetry. Her mind is analytical, and
      "her analyses, inordinately ordinate as they so victoriously
      are, subserve an end beyond analysis: their admirable el-
      bows admirably ad hoc, their high rearings and higher bolt-
      ings, their altogether porcupinity impeccable...."

15   _____. "Comment." The Dial, 78 (March), 265-68. Titled "The
      Footnotes of Marianne Moore" in the semiannual index.
          The scholarly notes which embellish Observations display
      in most cases a faithful erudition. But in one poem she
      forsakes learning for myth by perpetuating the by-science-
      not-substantiated story of catching unicorns in the lap of
      a virgin.

16   _____. "Comment." The Dial, 78 (April), 354-56. Titled "The
      Footnotes of Marianne Moore" in the semiannual index.
          Moore's footnotes in Observation display "copious erudi-
      tion." More important, they establish a new species of lit-
      erature--"the Footnotes of Aesthetic Ennoblement"--compared
      to which Eliot's efforts in the Waste Land are "small beer."
      Moore's footnote on Sir John Hawkins' deducing from an abun-
      dance of unicorns an abundance of lions (in "Sea Unicorns
      and Land Unicorns") is especially nice.

17 _____. "Announcement." The Dial, 78 (June), 532-34.
    Beginning with the next volume of the Dial, Moore will
    be the acting editor.

18 UNTERMEYER, LOUIS. "Marianne Moore." In his Modern American
    Poetry: A Critical Anthology. 3rd rev. ed. New York:
    Harcourt, Brace and Co., pp. 444-45.
    Largely because of "the physical pattern of her lines,"
    I agree with those who call Moore's "highly intellectualized
    dissertations" criticism rather than poetry. They are "a
    sort of witty and ironic geometry."

19 WESCOTT, GLENWAY. "Concerning Miss Moore's Observations." The
    Dial, 78 (January), 1-4.
    Moore's poetry presents experiences about which we other-
    wise would "remain in utter ignorance." It is "the product
    of a novel intelligence, a strange sensibility, a unique
    scholarship." Her "eccentric" mind exploits the environment,
    drawing from it not ornamentation but illustration. She has
    not called her observations poems, but in them are "passages
    of pure poetry, unmatched in American literature except by
    Poe." They seem to show the influence of Bacon, Sir Thomas
    Browne, or Burton. They are "the self-portrait of a mind.
    Although writing, like Joyce and Proust, in a baroque style,
    Moore is not indebted to them. And her work is sometimes
    more difficult than theirs.

20 WILLIAMS, WILLIAM CARLOS. "Marianne Moore." The Dial, 78
    (May), 393-401.
    Moore's poetry avoids connectives. It produces "the aes-
    thetic pleasure engendered where pure craftsmanship joins
    hard surfaces skilfully." The elements of her poetry--ap-
    ples, trees, thoughts, or whatever--are not distorted when
    they come together in her poems.
    Reprinted: 1925.21, 1932.2, 1954.30, 1966.24, 1969.28,
    1970.16.

*21 _____. "Marianne Moore." In his Contact Collection of Contem-
    porary Writers. Paris: Contact Editions, Three Mountains
    Press, pp. 326-38.
    Reprint of 1925.20. Listed in Emily Mitchell Wallace, A
    Bibliography of William Carlos Williams (Middletown, Conn.:
    Wesleyan University Press, 1968), p. 114.

22 WINTERS, YVOR. "'Holiday and Day of Wrath.'" Poetry, 26
    (April), 39-44.
    Moore is an "exacting moralist" whose readers are left
    either "dumbfounded" or "subjugated." One of her greatest

1926

achievements is the "transference of the metaphysical into
physical terms." Her poems are made of "scattered" or "log-
ical" sequences of images and ideas and often combine satire
with other moods. She has a fine sense of rhythm. I am
sure of her genius.
    Excerpted: 1960.17. Reprinted: 1973.17.

1926

1   MUNSON, GORHAM B. "In This Age of Hard Trying, Nonchalance Is
      Prejudiced." The Little Review, 12 (Spring-Summer), 54-58.
        Moore is "an amazing minor poet" who values precision
    rather than both precision and comprehensiveness. Her po-
    etry treats fragments of her experience, not its totality.
    She complacently views herself as an "imperfect instrument"
    of observation; she clings self-protectively to Victorian
    attitudes that dictate much of her style. But what she
    does, she does well. She purifies words, as Williams says.
    She has a fine and "peculiar" rhythm. She is witty. As a
    critic and editor, however, she is less successful.
        Reprinted: 1928.1.

1927

1   ANON. "The Decline of the Dial." The New Republic, 52 (12
      October), 211.
        The New Republic did not say (1927.2) that the Dial has
    failed to encourage any interesting new American writer,
    only that it is difficult to think of any. It has encour-
    aged Hart Crane, but it has rejected many others, including
    Yeats, whom it earlier printed. Moore, who is now the edi-
    tor of the Dial, seems not to be responsible for creating
    the magazine's policy, but she is continuing it. For a long
    time, the Dial has seemed nothing "more than a random throw-
    ing together of literary scraps."

2   ANON. "A Number of Things: The Dial Award." The New Republic,
      49 (5 January), 192.
        Awarding its prize for 1926 to Williams, the Dial contin-
    ues its practice of favoring writers whose popularity is
    already established and who therefore do not profit most
    from it. The recipients--Eliot, Van Wyck Brooks, Moore,
    Cummings, and now Williams--appeared in the Dial during
    1920, the "first year of its present phase." Few interesting
    new writers have appeared in it since then. (Gilbert Seldes

replies to this editorial in a letter in the 9 February
issue, p. 332. He does not mention Moore.)

3   RIDING, LAURA and ROBERT GRAVES. A Survey of Modernist Poetry.
    London: William Heinemann Ltd., pp. 111-13, 168, 185-86,
    249-50.
        Moore's "To a Steam Roller" assumes that the reader "is
    willing to part with the decayed flesh of poetry, the dete-
    riorated sentimental part, and to confine himself to the
    hard, matter-of-fact skeleton of poetic logic." "People's
    Surroundings" reflects the modernists' efforts to incorpo-
    rate in their art what previously were thought unpoetic
    subjects.

1928

1   MUNSON, GORHAM B. "Marianne Moore: In This Age of Hard Trying,
    Nonchalance Is Prejudiced." In his Destinations: A Canvass
    of American Literature since 1900. New York: J. H. Sears
    & Co., pp. 90-100.
        Reprint with minor revisions of 1926.1. Excerpted:
    1960.17.

1929

1   DRINKWATER, JOHN, HENRY SEIDEL CANBY, and WILLIAM ROSE BENÉT,
    eds. "Marianne Moore (1887-   )." Twentieth-Century Poetry.
    Cambridge, Mass.: Houghton Mifflin Co., pp. 577-78.
        Moore is a frustrated essayist whose failure to provide
    connectives renders her obscure. She is secretly religious
    and wears "an uncompromisingly stiff, flat, black hat over
    severely chastened red-gold hair."

2   KREYMBORG, ALFRED. "Originals and Eccentrics." In his Our
    Singing Strength: An Outline of American Poetry (1620-1930).
    New York: Coward-McCann, Inc., pp. 490-94.
        Moore, who has written little poetry since her rise from
    obscurity to the editorship of the Dial, cannot be accounted
    for: she is novel. Her poetry borrows phrases but is not
    "borrowed art." Her poems are visual, and rhymes give them
    "a fairly regular beat." Her English is American but aris-
    tocratic. Whether her work is poetry or not is beside the
    point. It is an art of "wit and wisdom," the product of a
    heart "under the control of a mind devoted to the impersonal,
    to reasoning and logic, to beauty evolved in cool detachment."

1929

3   SITWELL, EDITH. "Experiment in Poetry." In <u>Tradition and Ex-</u>
    <u>periment in Present-Day Literature: Addresses Delivered at</u>
    <u>the City Literary Institute.</u> London: Oxford University
    Press, pp. 87-90.
        Moore's "Black Earth" illustrates the vices (especially
    that of obscurity) and virtues (the form suited to sense)
    of modernist poetry. Her habit of ending lines with <u>of</u>, <u>a</u>,
    and <u>and</u> or in the middle of a word works in this poem but
    is "maddening" in others.

4   TATE, ALLEN. "American Poetry since 1920." <u>The Bookman</u>, 68
    (January), 506-507.
        Moore writes poetry marked by technical accomplishment
    but not informed by ideas. Her style is characterized by
    "precision of statement, decorative imagery, and a sense of
    the allusive value of nonsense phrases." No contemporary
    writer has surpassed the "technical perfection" of <u>Observa-</u>
    <u>tions</u>. Moore is a Victorian, with the Victorian ideas
    lacking but the corresponding feelings intact.

5   TAUPIN, RENÉ. "Marianne Moore." In his <u>L'Influence du sym-</u>
    <u>bolisme français sur la poésie Américaine (de 1910 a 1920)</u>.
    Paris: Librairie ancienne honoré champion, pp. 273-75.
        Although she had read neither Laforgue nor Rimbaud when
    she published her first poems in 1915, Moore nonetheless
    resembles them and Mallarmé in her gift for observation.
    She tends to use her observations as an illustration of a
    principle, of a moral, but the twentieth century does not
    allow a moral to be the reason for existence of an observa-
    tion. Thus she bases her art on irony and style. Like
    Laforgue, she creates a dance of words. Her techniques of
    diction and composition can be found in the French symbol-
    ists, especially Laforgue, but her poetry is original in its
    subjects.

<u>1931</u>

1   ZUKOFSKY, LOUIS. "American Poetry 1920-1930." <u>The Symposium</u>,
    2 (January), 61-62, 72-73, 76, 79.
        Like Pound, Williams, and Eliot, Moore "did not stop with
    the monolinear image"--indeed, never really started with the
    mere image. In "Unfinished Poem," Robert McAlmon has a
    scope and individualism but not an incisiveness that recall
    Moore's "An Octopus." Moore's "Fear Is Hope" ("Sun") is
    "worthy of John Donne."
        Excerpted in 1931.2.

12

2 ____. "Program: 'Objectivists' 1931." <u>Poetry</u>, 37 (February), 26.
Moore's <u>Observations</u> is among the "works absolutely necessary to students of poetry."
Reprints portion of 1931.1.

1932

1 WARD, ALFRED C. <u>American Literature, 1880-1930</u>. New York:
L. MacVeagh, Dial Press; London: Methuen & Co., pp. 196-99.
"Poetry" is a "modernist manifesto." It makes claims
not unlike those made "long ago" by Whitman. It is prose
cast as poetry and thus is more "sensational" and thus is
poetry. The form shocks one into attention.

*2 WILLIAMS, WILLIAM CARLOS. "Marianne Moore." In his A <u>Novel-</u>
<u>ette and Other Prose (1921-1931)</u>. [Toulouse]: TO
Publishers.
Reprint of 1925.20. Listed in Emily Mitchell Wallace,
<u>A Bibliography of William Carlos Williams</u> (Middletown, Conn.:
Wesleyan University Press, 1968), p. 30.

1934

1 AIKEN, CONRAD. "Personae." <u>Poetry</u>, 44 (August), 278.
Except for the poems by Williams and Moore, all of the
poems in the <u>Active Anthology</u> could have been written by
its editor, Ezra Pound.

2 PARSONS, I. M. "Active and Passive." <u>The Spectator</u>, 152 (12
January), 57.
Moore is "a competent descriptive poet," more interested
in "Natural History than in poetry." She is more "conservative" than the others represented in Pound's <u>Active</u>
<u>Anthology</u>.

1935

1 ANON. Brief notice of <u>Selected Poems</u>. <u>The Booklist</u>, 31
(July), 371.
<u>Selected Poems</u> contains "poetry of erudition and bright
imagery."

2 BENÉT, WILLIAM ROSE. "The Phoenix Nest." <u>The Saturday Review</u>
<u>of Literature</u>, 11 (23 March), 571.

1935

       More of an essayist than a poet, Moore writes poems that
can be read as peculiar conversations.

3   BLACKMUR, R. P. "The Method of Marianne Moore." In his The
       Double Agent: Essays in Craft and Elucidation. New York:
       Arrow Editions, pp. 141-71.
       In "The Past Is the Present," Moore uses inverted commas
to hold for examination "units of association," and through
a formal pattern of "elegant balances and compact understatement," she organizes and enlivens her material, of which the
pattern becomes a part. This poems also reminds us of the
Hebrew poetry that serves "as a background ideal" for her
poetry. The last line--"Ecstasy affords the occasion and
expediency determines the form"--is central to her poetic.
"Poetry" thus presents "carefully measured understatement
neatly placed among expedient ornament." She sets the quo-
tidian in the garden of imagination and shows it to be genuine. The Observations version of "Poetry" (Blackmur is
referring to the thirteen-line version that appears in the
second impression of Observations) fails--partly through a
lack of verbal technique, which in Moore is visual as well
as aural. In "Silence," the form is produced through
"heightened speech" and understatement. Analyses of "The
Monkey Puzzle," "The Steeple-Jack," "The Hero," "Nine Nectarines and Other Porcelain," and "An Octopus" further reveal
her method. The resemblance of some of Pound's cantos to
"An Octopus" may show Moore's influence. Moore's poetry
does not use "stirring" subjects or lines; she combines a
"romantic reticence" with a "fastidious thirst for detail."
       Reprinted: 1952.15, 1957.6, 1969.28.

4   BOGAN, LOUISE. "The Season's Verse." The New Yorker, 11 (4
       May), 66-67.
       Eliot's introduction to Selected Poems presents, in addi-
tion to "some of the most penetrating sentences on the poetic function ever written," an accurate assessment of Moore's
verse. In writing her poems, Moore "has not dissipated or
diffused herself."

5   BURKE, KENNETH. "Recent Poetry." The Southern Review, 1 (Sum-
       mer), 164-66.
       Moore's poems are "miniatures" that, though "expressing
a tiny corner of experience," have larger implications--
about, for example, the nature of poetry. The current eco-
nomic and political situation, the prevalence of "big bow
wow stuff," Moore's linguistic subtlety and "conversational
understatement"--these may make our reading of Moore difficult. But she does have, as Eliot says, genuineness.

1935

6   COON, ARTHUR. Review of <u>Selected Poems</u>. <u>Frontier and Midland</u>,
     15 (Summer), 324.
         Moore's poetry is largely "descriptive and intellectual"
     and "remarkable for its phonic delicacy."

7   DAVIDSON, EUGENE. "Some American Poets." <u>The Yale Review</u>, 24
     (June), 848.
         Eliot's introduction to <u>Selected Poems</u> offers high praise
     and forestalls negative criticism. The poems are witty,
     delicate in verse forms, too abundant in images, and fresh
     in perception. They are poems of the eye and mind.

8   ELIOT, T. S. "Introduction." In <u>Selected Poems</u> by Marianne
     Moore. New York: The Macmillan Co., pp. vii-xiv; London:
     Faber and Faber Ltd., pp. 5-12.
         Moore's poetry forms "part of the small body of durable
     poetry written in our time." It works to maintain the Eng-
     lish language. It is original--without any "immediate po-
     etic derivation," although there is a suggestion of H. D.'s
     influence in "A Talisman." Although it is descriptive and
     attentive to minute detail, it does not lack emotion. Moore
     is the "greatest living master" of light rhyme, which she
     uses in counterpoint to meter and sense.
         Reprinted: 1969.28.

9   EMERSON, DOROTHY. "Poetry Corner: Marianne Moore." <u>Scholastic</u>,
     27 (2 November), 11.
         Books are the raw material for Moore's unusual poetry.
     "Silence" and "No Swan So Fine" are typical in their use of
     description and figurative language.

10   HAWKINS, A. DESMOND. Review of <u>Selected Poems</u>. <u>The Criterion</u>,
     14 (July), 697-700.
         Like Eliot, Pound, and Williams, Moore avoids the "affec-
     tation of grandeur in manner" that has been evident through-
     out the Romantic decline. So too does she avoid mere "clum-
     sy revulsion" against poetry as "noble utterance." Her
     method is to set rhyme against rhythm and meaning and thus
     to establish "a discernable formal pattern, without the
     overblown echo of traditional metric."

11   JACK, PETER MONRO. "A Book of Selected Poems by Marianne
     Moore." <u>The New York Times Book Review</u>, 84 (28 April), 2.
         Moore's poems are "observations" that consist of "brightly
     colored images with meaningful and often moral connections."
     The images and connections give her an "authoritative tone"
     and provide a substitute for "spiritual certainty." She

1935

seems influenced by Henry James, if anyone. As "Poetry"
implies, she is in the American tradition and is allied with
Eliot and Cummings in a "new pragmatism of poetry."

12   JONES, GLYN. Review of Selected Poems. The Adelphi, series
3, 10 (July), 251-52.
Moore's poetry has a rich surface of detail. Her agility
in moving from one image to another is fascinating and does
not result "in rag-bag poetry." Moore controls her perceptions and embodies them in verse that "compels form and
organisation."

13   LEAVIS, F. R. "Marianne Moore." Scrutiny, 4 (June), 87-90.
I did not read much of Observations when it appeared, and
now I am left "defeated and exasperated" by Selected Poems.
Despite Eliot's introduction, I cannot "see the point" of
any of the poems. Moore's habit of quoting will not satisfy
readers who seek feeling in poetry; her concentration of
visual description suggests that she has chosen the wrong
medium. Her rhyme, at odds with sense, is irritating.

14   LECHLITNER, RUTH. "Poems of Fastidious Pattern." New York
Herald Tribune Books, 11 (2 June), 6.
Moore's unique verse has not drawn many readers--espe-
cially not those "who prefer an emotional simplicity to
intricate patterns of intellectual observation and association." Eliot's praise of Moore in his introduction to Selected Poems is deserved, partly because of her "metrical
originality" and even more because of her "gift for observation." Her later poems show more use of direct quota-
tion--a practice that can become irritating. Moore is "an
aristocratic precisionist."

15   PARSONS, I. M. "New Verse." The Spectator, 154 (26 April),
704.
Moore's poetry is genuine and, as Eliot says in his introduction to Selected Poems, serves the language. It is
neither too vague nor too eccentric. It is to be enjoyed
for its observations, not for revelations.

16   PELTZ, MARY ELLIS. "Iris." Voices, no. 83 (Autumn), pp. 45-47.
Selected Poems, with its erratic use of rhythms and
rhymes, will turn away those "used to melodic bardinage."

17   RICE, PHILIP BLAIR. "The Poetry of Fastidiousness." The
Nation, 140 (17 April), 458-60.
Moore's poems rely on but are not limited to visual im-
agery (especially of color and design). They "evoke a

physiological balance." Some of her early poems display
a conscious rather than unconscious fastidiousness. Her
more recent work in Selected Poems is not frigid, though
Eliot's statement that her poems "release the 'major emo-
tions'" is disputable.

18   SHUSTER, GEORGE N. "Recent Verse." The Commonweal, 22 (7
     June), 164.
          Selected Poems is "an absorbing and astonishingly intel-
     ligent book." Moore combines something of Donne with some-
     thing of "the keen archery of a modern American woman."

19   SMITH, A. J. M. "Observations." The Rocking-Horse, 2, no. 4
     (Summer), 26-29.
          Selected Poems contains "genuine poetry," neat and devoid
     of high-sounding nonsense. The poems express "with formal
     elegance" straightforward feelings. They fuse thought and
     feeling in image, narrative movement, and sound. Moore is
     superior to the imagists in "intellectual subtlety and
     strength."

20   STEVENS, WALLACE. "A Poet That Matters." Life and Letters
     To-day, 13 (December), 61-65.
          Selected Poems is not "merely fastidious": it is unaf-
     fected, witty, colloquial, and diverse. Light rhymes, syl-
     labic stanza patterns, visual arrangement, and relations of
     sounds and letters are used to good effect--as, for example,
     in "The Steeple-Jack," which also reveals Moore to be a poet
     who "leans to the romantic."
          Reprinted: 1957.29. See also 1966.23.

21   ZABEL, MORTON DAUWEN. "Marianne Moore." The New Republic, 83
     (7 August), 370.
          Selected Poems is the work of an observer whose vision is
     more complex than the poems it finally produces. Moore's
     reputation would not have survived if her work "rested on
     nothing but the strained intellection, the forced sophisti-
     cation, for which it is commonly dismissed."
          Reprinted: 1937.4.

1936

1   ANON. "Innovations in Poetry To-day: Miss Marianne Moore's
    Experiments." The Times Literary Supplement, no. 1772 (18
    January), p. 52.
         Eliot's introduction to Selected Poems "does not convince
    us that his admiration of Miss Moore's poetry has been based

1936

on a sufficiently exact apprehension of its principles."
One must understand technique, especially her syllabics.
"Peter" is an "apotheosis of syllabism." Its syllabic
scheme is thrown into relief by unobtrusive rhyme, and its
stanzas conflict with the sense of the poem. In "To Statecraft Embalmed," her technique is "brilliant," showing that
her "seeming casualness is part of a conscious plan." Like
Eliot and Pound, Moore engages in experiments that imply a
"revulsion for common life and common standards"--a revulsion that she carries to "elaborate lengths of exaltation."
Reprinted: 1957.4.

2   ANON. Review of The Pangolin and Other Verse. The Times Lit-
     erary Supplement, no. 1797 (11 July), p. 582.
        The animals of these five poems are fit subjects for
     "Moore's eclectic muse, her fastidious recall from the com-
     mon province of humanity." The poems are not as difficult
     as some of her earlier ones.

3   FINCH, JOHN. "Two Spokesmen for the Man Alone." The Sewanee
     Review, 44 (January-March), 122-25.
        Contemporary literature reflects the current formation of
     the opposing camps of collectivism and individualism. Like
     Cummings, Moore has chosen the way of the individualist.
     She writes with a deep wit out of which arise those features,
     such as "the subtle embroidery of quoted phrases," that mark
     her work as hers alone. She describes an object in such a
     way that its spiritual properties are intimated. Her van-
     tage point is original, if sometimes too distant for commu-
     nication with her readers. In Selected Poems, most success-
     ful are "A Grave," "The Jerboa," "Poetry," "Roses Only,"
     and "The Frigate Pelican."

4   LEWIS, MAY. "Marianne Moore: An Appreciation." Forum and
     Century, 96 (July), 48, ix.
        Moore's verse is more like a thicket to be observed than
     a velvet lawn on which to recline. Observed enough, it re-
     veals "delicate pagodas of thought" and so forth. Moore has
     the power of "seeing minutely" and "feeling through
     observation."

5   Z[ABEL], M[ORTON] D[AUWEN]. "A Literalist of the Imagination."
     Poetry, 47 (March), 326-36.
        Moore's admirers and detractors are actually close to
     agreement about the nature, if not the value, of her work.
     Her early and recent poems in Selected Poems have the same
     obvious traits: "a dispassionate accuracy of detail, liter-
     alness of manner, indifference to the standardized feelings

and forms of verse, and an admission that virtually any
subject-matter or reference is fully as appropriate to poetry as prose." Selected Poems omits some of her early, un-
conventionally imagistic works, such as "A Talisman." Her
most recent works are more complex, more elaborate in form,
more detailed--but still vigorous. She can see animals in
such a way that their appearance and meaning coincide, and
she is thus, in her phrase, a "literalist of the imagination."
She is not a poet of "disembodied emotion"; her poems must
be read as poems. A reading of "The Fish" reveals her method of making imagery, syntax, and stanzaic form interdepen-
dent. Her "novelty, eccentricity, and intellectual irony,"
which might seem obstacles, serve her poetic purposes.
Reprinted: 1937.4.

6   _____. "Poets of Five Decades." The Southern Review, 2 (Summer), 173-74.
Despite the unmatched complexity of her "presentation of
the modern intelligence and its problems," Moore "states
but never explains." Her ideas and method are implicit.
Her objectifications of animate and inanimate nature are a
private but "rigidly intellectual" system of symbolism. The
poems of The Pangolin and Other Verse are typical.

1937

1   BERTI, LUIGI. Review of Selected Poems. Letteratura, 1 (January), 164-67.
Moore's use of rhyme and of prose rhythms is an important
innovation in English poetry. Objects in her poems are
linked by a process of association. Her poems are difficult,
metaphysical. "The Fish" and "The Jerboa" are typical.

2   HORTON, PHILIP. Hart Crane: The Life of an American Poet.
New York: W. W. Norton & Co., pp. 95, 189-90, 208, 228.
"With the incredible editorial presumption for which she
was notorious," Moore insisted on radical revisions in
Crane's "The Wine Menagerie" before the Dial would accept
it. Later, knowing Moore's fondness for animals, Crane sent
her "Repose of Rivers."

3   WINTERS, YVOR. Primitivism and Decadence: A Study of American
Experimental Poetry. New York: Arrow Editions, pp. 7,
26-27, 35-36, 58-60, 91, 96, 107, 111-12, 115.
Moore is among the best poets writing so-called free
verse. Her "Black Earth" provides an example of one kind
of "pseudo-reference"; "My Apish Counsins" provides a

1937

contrast with another. As an ironist, she resembles "the
early Elizabethan epigrammatists," although in her later
work the irony "is developed through a very elaborate structure." Her virtues are certain intention, simultaneously
"magnificent and ironic" diction, and "control of an elaborate rhetoric." Her weaknesses are tendencies toward "a
rhetoric more complex than her matter," mere description,
and a view based more on manners than on morals. Moore and
Pound have "brought to its greatest perfection" the Whitman-
ian "long free-verse line." My free verse is indebted to
Moore, Williams, and Hopkins in its use of "run-over lines."
Moore's metric, with its long feet and thus long lines (e.g.,
in "A Grave"), produces a breathless movement contrasting
with the minute details of the subject matter or, in "Marriage" and "An Octopus," with the lack of a "coherent ratio-
nal frame."
Reprinted: 1947.6.

4   ZABEL, MORTON DAUWEN. "A Literalist of the Imagination." In
his Literary Opinion in America: Essays Illustrating the
Status, Methods, and Problems of Criticism in the United
States since the War. New York: Harper & Brothers, pp.
426-36.
Reprint of 1935.21 and 1936.5. Excerpted: 1960.17.

1938

1   MONROE, HARRIET. "Discoveries." In her A Poet's Life: Seventy Years in a Changing World. New York: Macmillan Co.,
p. 393.
Poetry "introduced...the elliptically whimsical profundi-
ties of Marianne Moore."

1940

1   DREW, ELIZABETH and JOHN L. SWEENEY. Directions in Modern Poetry. New York: W. W. Norton, pp. 64-69, 75, 106, 182,
195, 200, 233, 242, 257, 258, 269, 270-71.
There never will be a large audience for Moore's poetry,
since she does not speak directly to "general humanity."
Her remoteness is part of "an instinctive aristocratic qui-
etism." Moore uses quotations for their substance rather
than their allusiveness.
Excerpted: 1960.17.

2   LUIGI, BERTI. "Approccio per Marianne Moore." In his
    Boccaporto. Firenze: Parenti, pp. 193-98.
        Reprint of 1937.1.

3   MILLET, FRED B. Contemporary American Authors: A Critical
    Survey and 219 Bio-Bibliographies. New York: Harcourt,
    Brace and Co., pp. 144-45, 491-92.
        Moore's poetry might be regarded as "rhythmic prose that
    has been submitted to a rather freakish system of lineation."
    Her metaphors are fresh and extravagant. Includes brief
    biography and bibliography.

1941

1   ANON. "Books Received." The Christian Century, 58 (8 October),
    1243.
        As What Are Years shows, Moore is a "poet's poet." Her
    work is subtle, delicate, sometimes unintelligible. Breaking
    words between lines "is a mannerism she probably mistakes for
    a merit."

2   ANON. "Selected for Poetry Award." The New York Times, 11
    January, p. 5.
        It was announced yesterday that Moore has won the Poetry
    Society of America's Shelley Award.

3   BOGAN, LOUISE. "Verse." The New Yorker, 17 (1 November),
    71-72.
        What Are Years continues Moore's civilized, "austere
    manner." Her poems are marked by an extraordinary formality
    and "imaginative richness." Moore is neither sentimental
    nor surreal.

4   BRUNINI, JOHN GILLAND. "Book Reviews." Spirit, 8 (November),
    163-64.
        To write the poems of What Are Years would require "a
    strange mind" whose reputation is "more accepted than exam-
    ined" and who writes esoteric lines that merely look like
    poetry.

5   CARGILL, OSCAR. Intellectual America: Ideas on the March.
    New York: The Macmillan Co., pp. 299-304.
        Moore's familiarity with the "Decadents" led her to be-
    lieve in "novelty for its own sake," which she has sought
    "with extraordinary perseverance." Added to that belief is
    the "rigorous discipline" picked up at Bryn Mawr, which was
    "presided over by such female martinets and pedants as

1941

M. Carey Thomas...and Mrs. Grace Frank." Moore's fastidiousness is conscious, but her "cultivated passion" makes
poetry of her statements. She lacks an ear. Her splitting
of infinitives and her weak lines show that she is not "the
meticulous craftsman" she is said to be. Her imagery, however, is "the true stuff of verse."

6   COLUM, MARY M. "The New Books of Poetry." The New York Times
     Book Review, 30 November, p. 20.
          In What Are Years, as in her other work, Moore has a
     unique style. Does she write poetry? Only according to
     one definition—Gautier's statement that poets are those who
     see the exterior world. I do not think that some of her
     pieces are poems, although there is "something achieved and
     real" in all of them. Moore is really a fabulist.

7   COWLEY, MALCOLM. "Three Poets." The New Republic, 105 (10
     November), 625.
          Moore is at once an impersonal and individual poet. She
     has discovered and remained faithful to a prosody that ne-
     glects accents and counts syllables and to a subject matter
     "of small animals or inanimate things." Her poems typically
     present observation that becomes a statement about human
     destiny. What Are Years is further evidence that "she
     prints nothing that fails to meet her own rigorous standards."

8   FRANKENBERG, LLOYD. "The Book of the Years." Decision, 2,
     nos. 5-6 (November-December), 115-17.
          Every poem in What Are Years reflects some part of Moore's
     genius. Her poetry is characterized by freedom within form
     and by the coincidence of ornament and function. Her syl-
     labic meter allows her to incorporate spoken rhythms—or
     any rhythms—and still have the tension between rhythm and
     form that distinguishes poetry from prose.

9   GREENBERG, CLEMENT. "Two Poets." The Nation, 153 (13 Decem-
     ber), 616-17.
          Moore has a deficiency of energy. Like other first-gen-
     eration modernist poets in America, she lacks "cultural
     capital." Her sensibility is "too private," and despite
     its fondness for deducing morals, it "makes only aesthetic
     discriminations." Her predilections, lacking external con-
     trol, are indiscriminate. But the poetry of this "feminine
     odd American young poetess" still delights. The recent po-
     ems in What Are Years introduce "apothegms and moralizations"
     that are not "quite so arch or so cute" as her earlier work.

10   KUNITZ, STANLEY J. "The Pangolin of Poets." <u>Poetry</u>, 59 (No-
     vember), 96-98.
          <u>What Are Years</u> will add to the pleasure of Moore's read-
     ers. Her attention to detail, her rhythms that are prose
     rhythms extended, her largely visual rhyme and stanza
     schemes, her serenity in an age when "poetry is largely a
     cry of confusion and anguish," her clean but cluttered mind
     --they are all there.
          Reprinted: 1975.7.

11   LECHLITNER, RUTH. "Fastidious Poetic Craftsman." <u>New York
     Herald Tribune Books</u>, 18 (23 November), 6.
          Moore has a "comparatively restricted audience." She
     won the Shelley Award for 1940 but has been honored less
     than she deserves. Her "technical mastery, fastidious wit,
     intellectual sensibility and gift of creative scholarship
     --all seen in <u>What Are Years</u>--" make her a major poet of
     our time.

12   UNTERMEYER, LOUIS. "Time and These Times." <u>The Yale Review</u>,
     31 (December), 377.
          <u>What Are Years</u> contains some of Moore's "most exact--and
     most exacting--studies." For the first time, she has sup-
     plied "A Note on the Notes." The most original poet, Moore
     is also the most indebted to other authors, whose work she
     incorporates in her own. "...I once spoke of Miss Moore's
     work as a sort of witty geometry. I should like to change
     the mathematical image, for her poems owe more to Lyly and
     even Spenser than they do to Euclid. This poet is at her
     best in reflections of her reading, twisting the phrases
     about in a kind of analyzed memory, a microscopic musing."

<u>1942</u>

1   ANON. "Moore, Marianne Craig." In <u>Twentieth Century Authors:
     A Biographical Dictionary of Modern Literature</u>. Edited by
     Stanley J. Kunitz and Howard Haycraft. New York: The H.
     Wilson Co., pp. 979-80.
          Biographical sketch that includes statements by Moore.
          <u>See also</u> 1955.3.

2   BURKE, KENNETH. "Motives and Motifs in the Poetry of Marianne
     Moore." <u>Accent</u>, 2 (Spring), 157-69.
          Moore's poetry establishes "a relationship between the
     external and internal, or visible and invisible, or back-
     ground and personality." Too descriptive to be called Sym-
     bolist, her poetry is closer to that of Williams and

1942

> objectivism, though one discerns a principle of appreciation
> at work in her choice of objectively presented details. De-
> tails are appraised as things themselves but also exist "as
> objective replica of the subjective." Illustrative are her
> poems "People's Surroundings," "Spenser's Ireland," "What
> Are Years," "Sojourn in the Whale," "The Fish," "Black
> Earth," "Half Deity," and "Bird-Witted." Seen in their
> progress through her poems, her motifs become motivated
> acts.
> Reprinted: 1945.5, 1946.4, 1968.15, 1969.28.

3   JARRELL, RANDALL. "The Country Was." Partisan Review, 9 (Jan-
     uary-February), 58-60.
        Parody of Moore's poetry.

4   _____. "The Humble Animal." The Kenyon Review, 4 (Autumn),
     408-11.
        Louis Untermeyer has foolishly said that Moore's poetry
     is actually criticism. Her poetry combines the virtues of
     poetry with the virtues of good prose. Her elaborate and
     arbitrary forms become the vehicle of emotion; her style
     allows her to say what she wants. She uses relations be-
     tween disparate objects. Like Henry James, she represents
     "a morality divorced from both religion and economics."
        Reprinted: 1951.9, 1953.13.

1943

1   MILLER, MARY OWINGS. "Poets of Today: Marianne Moore." Con-
     temporary Poetry, 3, no. 2 (Summer), 4.
        Moore's poetry springs from her power of observation and
     association. She has made "a distinct addition to prosody."
     Her poetry is demanding. (Quotes from a letter from Moore
     about her stanza rather than line as basic unit and about
     her fondness for unaccented rhyme.)

2   SWEENEY, JOHN L. "Burd-Alone." Furioso, 2, no. 1, 39-42.
        What Are Years is "more sombre in tone" and less epigram-
     matic than Observations. Moore has mastered the technique
     of the close-up. She submerges her rhymes "in her rhythms
     [,] which are those of intensified but natural speech." Her
     tone is modest, self-reliant, firm.

1944

1   ANON. "Books—Authors." The New York Times, 27 December,
        p. 17.
           The University of Chicago's Harriet Monroe Poetry Prize
        was awarded to Moore.

2   ANON. "Books Received." The Christian Century, 61 (22 Novem-
        ber), 1355.
           Nevertheless is a small book of subtle and skillful poems
        by a poet who is praised by Eliot, Pound, and Cummings.

3   AUDEN, W. H. "New Poems." The New York Times Book Review, 15
        October, pp. 7, 20.
           Ten years ago, when I first tried to read Moore, I could
        not, because her work was unique. Even today no other poet
        of Moore's stature is so little read. "I have already stolen
        a great deal" from her. "In Distrust of Merits," in Never-
        theless, is the best war poem.

4   BOGAN, LOUISE. "Verse." The New Yorker, 20 (11 November),
        88–89.
           Nevertheless is Moore's best book so far. In the years
        since Eliot's introduction to Selected Poems, Moore "has
        become both 'musical' and more openly warm-hearted." She
        avoids the "wistfulness" and "self-pity" that afflict some
        women writers. Her "poems are like fables." She is "our
        most distinguished American poet."
           Reprinted: 1955.10, 1970.4.

5   BRUNINI, JOHN GILLAND. "Book Reviews." Spirit, 11 (November),
        146–47.
           Nevertheless is a slim volume for Moore's "extreme cult."
        The book contains one good poem—"In Distrust of Merits,"
        which is as "typographically tortured" as the others but
        not as coldly and inconsequentially precise.

6   DREW, ELIZABETH. "The Vision beyond War." New York Herald
        Tribune Weekly Book Review, 21 (22 October), 3.
           Nevertheless contains those qualities of Moore's poetry
        that Eliot discerned, but it differs from her earlier work
        in its emotional warmth. "In Distrust of Merits" is the
        finest war poem I know.

7   DUPEE, F. W. "Verse Chronicle." The Nation, 159 (23 December),
        780.
           The seven recent poems in Nevertheless confirm Moore's
        "astonishing repute."

25

1944

8   WILLIAMS, OSCAR. "Ladies' Day." The New Republic, 111 (23
       October), 534.
         In Nevertheless, "our highly esteemed" Moore sticks "to
       the niche of syllabic patterns she has created for herself."
       "In Distrust of Merits" is "one of the finest war poems."

1945

1   ANON. "Christmas Stories." The New Yorker, 21 (8 December),
       136.
         Rock Crystal is beautifully translated.

2   AUDEN, W. H. "Concerning the Village of Gschaid, And Its Moun-
       tain." The New York Times Book Review, 18 November, p. 6.
         Rock Crystal is the first of the Adalbert Stifter's works
       to appear in English. The translation by Moore and Elizabeth
       Mayer "reads like the original."

3   BINSSE, HARRY LORIN. "Children's Books." The Commonweal, 43
       (16 November), 125.
         Rock Crystal is an appropriately slow-moving story con-
       taining the Christian spirit of Christmas.

4   BLACKMUR, R. P. "Notes on Eleven Poets." The Kenyon Review,
       7 (Spring), 341-43.
         Moore knows the value of counting. Her syllabic meter
       counterpoints her rhythm and serves to display and bring
       into focus her perceptions. Because her metric is "more
       conscious" than H. D.'s and Williams', it is "more flexible."

5   BURKE, KENNETH. "Motives and Motifs in the Poetry of Marianne
       Moore." In his A Grammar of Motives. New York: Prentice-
       Hall, Inc., pp. 485-502.
         Reprint of 1942.2.

6   DEVLIN, DENIS. Review of Nevertheless. The Sewanee Review,
       53 (Summer), 465.
         "In Distrust of Merits" is the poem of Moore's sudden
       confrontation with "the garish sinful world" that she had
       always avoided. "The Mind Is an Enchanting Thing" is more
       typical of her. It is a "delighting pattern" of superfici-
       alities and of trivialized or domesticated things.

7   HARTLEY, MARSDEN. "Marianne Moore." In his Selected Poems.
       Edited by Henry W. Wells. New York: The Viking Press,
       p. 107.
         Poem.

1946

8 HAYAKAWA, S. I. "Mind and Matter." Poetry, 65 (February), 262-64.
Moore collects observations, stores them, then arranges them into patterns that give rise to moral abstraction. One fine poem in Nevertheless, "In Distrust of Merits," speaks directly of her feelings about the war.

9 JARRELL, RANDALL. "Poetry in War and Peace." Partisan Review, 12 (Winter), 120-22.
Reviewers now see Moore less as a poet than as an institution, but her poetry, including that in Nevertheless, can be talked about. Her method is "an illogical atomism." Her syllabics and rhyme fix her particulars, making her poems static rather than dynamic. She finds values in culture and nature but ignores the unpleasant side of them. In "In Distrust of Merits" she gives up the particulars for abstraction and sees the war in "blindingly moral terms."

10 M. G. D. "A Story of Faith." The Saturday Review of Literature, 28 (8 December), 42.
Elizabeth Mayer and Moore's translation of Rock Crystal is "poetical and satisfying."

11 ROSENFELD, PAUL. "Under the Northern Lights." The Saturday Review of Literature, 28 (3 November), 11.
Moore and Elizabeth Mayer have made a fine translation of Rock Crystal, a realistic story about man's relationship with the cosmos.

12 SAPIEHA, VIRGILIA. "We Turn toward Home." New York Herald Tribune Book Review, 22 (16 December), 2.
Rock Crystal is rendered by its translators into "limpid prose."

1946

1 ANON. "Books and Authors." The New York Times, 16 May, p. 19.
Moore has received a grant of $1000 from the American Academy of Arts and Letters.

2 BREIT, HARVEY. "The Case for the Modern Poet." The New York Times, 3 November, sec. 6, pp. 20, 58, 60, 61.
Coblentz (1946.5) is wrong about modern poetry. Moore's poetry is precise and elegant. Its appearance on the page has to do with "movement, rhythm and sense," not with decoration.

1946

3   BRINNIN, JOHN MALCOLM. "Marianne Moore's." <u>Accent,</u> 6 (Spring),
     191-92.
         Poem.

4   BURKE, KENNETH. "Motives and Motifs in the Poetry of Marianne
     Moore." In <u>Accent Anthology: Selections from</u> Accent, <u>A</u>
     <u>Quarterly of New Literature, 1940-1945</u>. Edited by Kerker
     Quinn and Charles Shattuck. New York: Harcourt, Brace and
     Co., pp. 529-47.
         Reprint of 1942.2.

5   COBLENTZ, STANTON A. "What Are They--Poems or Puzzles?" <u>The</u>
     <u>New York Times Magazine,</u> 13 October, p. 51.
         Much modern poetry is not poetry. Moore wins prizes, but
     the freakish appearance of her work is its "only point of
     distinction."
         <u>See</u> 1946.2.

6   FRANKENBERG, LLOYD. "Meaning in Modern Poetry." <u>The Saturday</u>
     <u>Review of Literature,</u> 29 (23 March), 5.
         Poetry is condensed imagination, as in the meeting of the
     ideas of liberation and imprisonment in the word <u>steels</u> in
     Moore's "What Are Years."

7   GREGORY, HORACE and MARYA ZATURENSKA. "Marianne Moore: The
     Genius of <u>The Dial</u>." In their <u>A History of American Poetry</u>,
     <u>1900-1940</u>. New York: Harcourt, Brace and Co., pp. 317-35.
         Moore's method in <u>Selected Poems</u> was "to observe and then
     to comment briefly." More important than her method was her
     "air of courtesy and good breeding" with which she offered
     her observations. Democracy did not demand of her, as it
     did for many others in the 1920s, the sacrifice of dignity.
     Moore's fascination with animals and objects sometimes
     threatens the unity of her poetry.

8   HOFFMAN, FREDERICK J., CHARLES ALLEN, and CAROLYN F. ULRICH.
     <u>The Little Magazine: A History and a Bibliography</u>. Prince-
     ton: Princeton University Press, pp. 37, 48, 199-201.
         Moore was among the earlier contributors to <u>Poetry</u>. She
     was among those who occasionally met in Alfred Kreymborg's
     apartment in 1915 and who appeared in <u>Others</u>. During these
     early years "before she began writing her acid, almost prosy
     dissertations" her "work was faster reading." But as early
     as 1915, she did employ "the bizarre image, the juxtaposition
     of the abstract with the concrete, the wit, the irony, and
     satire, the profusion of rare and esoteric knowledge, and a
     sharp-cracking cacophony." After 1925, she "took much of
     the responsibility" for editing the <u>Dial</u>.

9   LINDQUIST, JENNIE D.   Brief notice of <u>Rock Crystal</u>.   <u>Library</u>
     <u>Journal</u>, 71 (1 January), 58.
         The translation is "excellent."

                            <u>1947</u>

1   ANON.   "More about Moore."   <u>Senior Scholastic</u>, 50 (28 April),
     15.
         Moore's poetry is a sort of precise "mosaic" of facts.
     She is fond of sports.   In her museum-like Brooklyn apart-
     ment, "she lives withdrawn, like an anchorite."   Her mind
     is crammed but neat.

2   ANON.   "Twelve Elected to Arts Institute."   <u>The New York Times</u>,
     3 January, p. 23.
         Moore was one of twelve new members elected yesterday to
     the National Institute of Arts and Letters.

3   COLE, THOMAS.   "To Marianne Moore."   <u>Interim</u>, 3, no. 1, 35-36.
         Poem.

*4   GLATSTEIN, JACOB.   <u>In Tokh Genumen: Essays, 1945-1947</u>.   New
     York: Farlag Matones.
         Though her art is personal, Moore builds poems in the
     tradition of American engineering.   Unlike Eliot and Pound,
     she did not revolt against America but conducted an American
     revolt.   She extends the range of poetic diction by using
     commonplace, unpoetic words.   Her poetry is characterized by
     visual rather than aural rhyme, humor, and quotation.   The
     conversation during my visit with her resembled one of her
     poems, and through it I discovered the influence of her
     mother, the moral base of her art, and the sympathy she has
     for the Jews.
         Not seen; abstract based on translation in 1973.8.

5   Le BRETON, MAURICE.   "Marianne Moore."   In his <u>Anthologie de</u>
     <u>la poésie américaine contemporaine</u>.   Paris: Les Éditions
     Denoël, p. 243.
         Moore is representative of the spirit of the Midwest.
     Her poetry is original--even eccentric--and is little influ-
     enced by the traditions that paralyzed American poetry before
     1912.   She is like Emily Dickinson.

1947

6   WINTERS, YVOR. <u>Primitivism and Decadence</u>. In his <u>In Defense</u>
     <u>of Reason</u>. Denver: The University of Denver Press, a Swal-
     low Press Book, pp. 41, 49-50, 70-71, 101, 104, 106, 116,
     120-21, 124.
          Reprint of 1937.3.

                          <u>1948</u>

1   BISHOP, ELIZABETH. "As We Like It: Miss Moore and the Delight
     of Imitation, Miss Moore and Edgar Allan Poe, Miss Moore and
     Zoography." <u>Quarterly Review of Literature</u>, 4, Marianne
     Moore Issue, 129-35.
          Moore is "The World's Greatest Living Observer." Her ac-
     curate descriptions seem at times compulsive, implying a
     duty to love and honor the things described. She heeds Poe's
     warning that one must employ metaphor carefully. She has
     acknowledged that Poe's prose has been an influence on her.
     It almost might be said that she "is Poe's Ideal Poet"--in
     her "truth telling," wide reading, and technical virtuosity.
     At times, out of modesty, she seems to use her "verse forms
     and rhyme schemes and syllabic logarithms" to make her task
     more difficult. Moore's feeling for animals is not conde-
     scending. Like the Chinese, she presents animals unroman-
     tically, democratically.

2   _____. "For M. M." <u>Quarterly Review of Literature</u>, 4, Mari-
     anne Moore Issue, 127-28.
          Poem.

3   BOGAN, LOUISE. "American Timeless." <u>Quarterly Review of Lit-</u>
     <u>erature</u>, 4, Marianne Moore Issue, 150-52.
          In Moore, seventeenth-century humanism and protestantism
     meet. She has a seventeenth-century "passion for miscellany"
     that sets her the "task of imaginatively correlating the
     world's goods, natural and artificial." And she writes po-
     ems that resemble Protestant plain-style sermons.

4   BROOKS, CLEANTH. "Miss Marianne Moore's Zoo." <u>Quarterly Re-</u>
     <u>view of Literature</u>, 4, Marianne Moore Issue, 178-83.
          Moore uses animals in her poetry to provide a perspective
     on our human world. In "Elephants," she does not use the
     elephant "patronizingly" as a figure in a simple moral alle-
     gory. Instead, the qualities of the elephant "are given a
     human reference." Central to her poetry is a "special blend
     of seriousness and humor" that can be seen in "The Jerboa,"
     in which the contrast between the Pharaoh and rat is not
     allowed to become precious or solemn.

1948

5   DILLON, GEORGE. "Excellence Is Baffling." <u>Quarterly Review</u>
    <u>of Literature</u>, 4, Marianne Moore Issue, 190-91.
        Moore's poetry, "which reviews God," is truthful, urbane,
    charming, and sometimes tiring in its excellence. Her crit-
    icism is scrupulous.

6   FOWLIE, WALLACE. "Under the Equanimity of Language." <u>Quarter-</u>
    <u>ly Review of Literature</u>, 4, Marianne Moore Issue, 173-77.
        <u>Nevertheless</u> demonstrates that through reflection "Moore
    has attained...the equanimity of language." Each poem im-
    plies "a silence on many other possible poems." "Elephants"
    and "In Distrust of Merits" reveal her method. For her,
    poetry is an "opportunity to transmit order from chaos."

7   FRANKENBERG, LLYOD. "The Imaginary Garden." <u>Quarterly Review</u>
    <u>of Literature</u>, 4, Marianne Moore Issue, 192-223.
        Moore uses the seen as a symbol of the unseen. Yet the
    two--image and idea--are fused. Even her poems of idea are
    more than the essays some have called them, since her ideas,
    heightened by emotion, take on an objectivity close to that
    of the image. She combines "sensation, thought, and emotion."
    Hers is an "imagination articulated by fact." Her observa-
    tions show correspondences between the mind observing and
    the thing observed (as is evident in "The Jerboa" and "The
    Frigate Pelican"). As she says in "Poetry," the art lies
    not in experience but in the use one makes of experience.
    Moore's metric--in "Bird-Witted," for example--distinguishes
    her poetry from prose and coincides with her content, espe-
    cially with "her constant theme" of "the resolution of op-
    posites, of necessities and freedom."
        Reprinted: 1949.2.

8   KOCH, VIVIENNE. "The Peaceable Kingdom of Marianne Moore."
    <u>Quarterly Review of Literature</u>, 4, Marianne Moore Issue,
    153-69.
        Moore is "in the tradition of the great fabulists," but
    she discovers moral qualities in correspondences between
    animal and human beings, not by having animals act out human
    dramas. She is like a novelist of manners--but of manners
    translated to "the animal sphere" and "didactically charged."
    Moore's "aesthetic becomes an ethic." Her poetry shows an
    influence of Hebrew poetry in her use of verbs of action and
    in poetic structure. And it shows the interests of a li-
    brarian. In <u>What Are Years</u> and <u>Nevertheless</u>, which show
    Moore's interest in American materials, there is a more
    obvious didacticism, "a greater lyricism of mood," and a
    more pronounced strain of protestant individualism. Moore

31

1948

is like La Fontaine but is intent more on illuminating than on instructing. And she is intent on extending her sensibility into an "imaginary animal kingdom of the soul and intellect."
Reprinted: 1950.1.

9   MATTHIESSEN, F. O. "Poetry." In Literary History of the United States. Edited by Robert E. Spiller et al. New York: The Macmillan Co., II, 1352-53.
    Moore's is a poetry of observation and has been called "objectivist" by Kenneth Burke. Moore "is feminine in a very rewarding sense, in that she makes no effort to be major." Her syllabic versification is unique. (Volume 3, pp. 662-63, contains a brief bibliography.)

10 O'CONNOR, WILLIAM VAN. Sense and Sensibility in Modern Poetry. Chicago: The University of Chicago Press, pp. 58-60, 75-76, 93, 116, 167, 170, 176, 229-30, 232-33.
    Moore's poetry does not present the objective world distorted by imagination. Her writing is prose heightened to poetry. "What Are Years" shows the tendency of modern poetry to use "associational and subsidiary meanings."

11 RAIZISS, SONA. "Marianne Moore." In La poésie américaine "moderniste," 1910-1940. Translated by Charles Cestre. Paris: Mercure de France, pp. 100-107.
    Moore's observations of things are precise and expressive. Moore is a poet of almost ecstatic objectivity. Her prosody is unique and subtle, crossing prose with poetry. She presents ideas through objects rather than about them. Her rhyme and meter are as subtle as her interpretations are implicit. As Eliot says in his introduction to Selected Poems (1935.8), her poetry is metaphysical in its associative description, but it lacks the passion of conflict found in true metaphysical poetry. There is in her work an animistic tendency: she penetrates the lives of things with her microscopic vision.

12 RANSOM, JOHN CROWE. "On Being Modern with Distinction." Quarterly Review of Literature, 4, Marianne Moore Issue, 136-42.
    Moore's poetry has been received with difficulty because of its modernity that challenges one's definition of poetry. Though her art is original, it is "one of the consequences ...of the Imagist cult of thirty years ago," especially of its efforts to "secularize or de-solemnize" poetry. Eliot, who has followed "the Symbolist way of poetry," raises in his introduction to Selected Poems (1935.8) the question of

the greatness of her work, but greatness is "beyond the
intention of her kind" of poetry, a poetry of "minor not
major effects." Her poem "He 'Digesteth Harde Yron'" is
technically daring, jostling metered verse against free.
Reprinted: 1969.28.

13   STEVENS, WALLACE. "About One of Marianne Moore's Poems."
      Quarterly Review of Literature, 4, Marianne Moore Issue,
      143-52.
          In his essay "On Poetic Truth," H. D. Lewis provides terms
      that aid in a discussion of Moore. Lewis distinguishes be-
      tween "isolated fact" and "individual reality." In Moore's
      "He 'Digesteth Harde Yron,'" there is "an aesthetic integra-
      tion" that is "individual reality." Moore is not interested
      in the ostrich as fact, nor in the poem as a mere vehicle of
      meaning. She digests "the 'harde yron' of appearance" in a
      way that suggests the method of a poetry that may contain
      "a reality adequate to the profound necessities of life
      today."
      Reprinted: 1951.12, 1969.28.

14   SWEENEY, JOHN L. "Poetic Power." Quarterly Review of Litera-
      ture, 4, Marianne Moore Issue, 170-72
          Moore's poetry, with its wit and "vein of enquiry," is
      speculative, like and unlike William Empson's. At the heart
      of her poetry are "sincerity and taste and 'poetic power.'"

15   WEBER, BROM. Hart Crane: A Biographical and Critical Study.
      New York: Bodley Press, pp. 35, 130, 135, 252, 253.
          As editor of the Dial, Moore rejected Crane's "Passage"
      because it lacked what she called "cumulative force." In a
      "feat of editorial arrogance," she accepted his "The Wine
      Menagerie" with the provision that the title be changed and
      numerous lines be deleted. Crane agreed only because he
      needed money.

16   WILLIAMS, WILLIAM CARLOS. "Marianne Moore." Quarterly Review
      of Literature, 4, Marianne Moore Issue, 125-26.
          I have cherished Moore's name "for nearly forty years."
      Her talent "diminishes the tom-toming on the hollow men of
      a wasteland to an irrelevant pitter-patter." The whole
      world is alive to her imagination; she discovers relation-
      ships in the world, even when she focuses on small objects.
      There is not "a better poet writing in America today."
      Reprinted: 1954.16, 1969.28.

1948

17   WILSON, T. C. "Strong Enchantment." <u>Quarterly Review of Lit-</u>
     <u>erature</u>, 4, Marianne Moore Issue, 184-89.
         Moore believes that "creative activity entails ethical
     and moral as well as esthetic responsibilities." She con-
     siders hope, fortitude, and humility indispensable qualities.

                              1949

1   ANON. "News Notes." <u>Poetry</u>, 74 (August), 308.
         "Moore has received the honorary degree of Doctor of
     Letters from Wilson College, Pennsylvania."

2   FRANKENBERG, LLOYD. "Marianne Moore's Imaginary Garden." In
     his <u>Pleasure Dome: On Reading Modern Poetry</u>. Boston:
     Houghton Mifflin Co., pp. 119-55.
         Reprint of 1948.7. Excerpted: 1960.17.

3   SYLVESTER, WILLIAM A. "Moore's 'The Fish.'" <u>The Explicator</u>,
     7 (February), item 30.
         The central image of "The Fish" is the injured fan. It
     embodies the opposed concepts of life and destruction, which
     contrast with the "placid mood" of the poem.

                              1950

1   KOCH, VIVIENNE. "The Peaceable Kingdom of Marianne Moore."
     <u>Poetry Quarterly</u>, 12 (Spring), 47-61.
         Reprint of 1948.8.

2   POUND, EZRA. <u>The Letters of Ezra Pound, 1907-1941</u>. Edited by
     D. D. Paige. New York: Harcourt, Brace and Co., pp. 60,
     135, 141-44, 146-48, 157, 165, 167-68, 173, 182, 184, 197,
     235-36, 238, 241, 244, 248, 259, 286, 295.
         Contains many references to Moore and four letters to
     her. Several are of especial interest. A letter to Moore,
     16 December 1918, criticizes "A Graveyard" and "Old Tiger"
     for language and line division, praises her work for holding
     his eye, asks about French influence, punctuation, and her
     life, and identifies her metric as syllabic. A letter to
     Williams, 18 March 1922, mentions Moore as a possible candi-
     date for Pound's Bel Esprit project. A letter to Harriet
     Monroe, 6 October 1931, says that only Moore could take
     over editorship of <u>Poetry</u>.

1   ANON. "Best Living Poet." <u>Newsweek</u>, 38 (24 December), 69-71.
    Moore is "probably the best living American poet," even
    though until recently she has been little known to the gen-
    eral public. Despite her reputation for difficult poems
    and reclusive life, her poems are "readily comprehensible,"
    by line if not by whole, and her life has not really been
    that of a recluse.

2   ANON. "Poems for the Eye." <u>Time</u>, 58 (10 December), 112
    "Just about the most accomplished poetess alive," Moore
    now offers her <u>Collected Poems</u> to her "small but fervent
    public." Her poems are about animals and humans. They are
    marked by restraint and are written for the eye as well as
    ear.

3   ANON. "Poetry Notes." <u>The Saturday Review of Literature</u>, 34
    (29 December), 12.
    Moore is an experimentalist who knows what she is doing.
    Her <u>Collected Poems</u> contains poems that are "satirical dis-
    quisitions." Though not obscure, she is difficult and not
    likely to be popular.

4   ANON. "Unconventional Poet." <u>The Times Literary Supplement</u>,
    no. 2,600 (30 November), p. 767.
    Moore's historical importance is undoubted. Her later
    work in <u>Collected Poems</u> shows little change in her "tech-
    nique of objective description and Imagist precision." Her
    powers of observation and epigram are not usually matched,
    however, by intensity or significance. Some of her poems
    (e.g., "Plumet Basilisk" and "Nine Nectarines") are obscure
    and are made more so in <u>Collected Poems</u> by Moore's revisions.

5   BOGAN, LOUISE. <u>Achievement in American Poetry, 1900-1950</u>.
    Chicago: Henry Regnery Co., pp. 57, 59, 61-62, 72, 76, 100,
    101, 102, 105.
    Moore combines "the attributes of the naturalist with
    those of a philosophical moralist." In its syllabics and
    hidden rhyme, her form is unique. Poems of her middle period
    are more colorful; those of the later (after 1941) are more
    direct and warmer.

6   BROWER, REUBEN ARTHUR. "Saying One Thing and Meaning Another."
    In his <u>The Fields of Light: An Experiment in Critical
    Reading</u>. New York: Oxford University Press, pp. 48-50.
    Moore's "Roses Only" is "a triumph of calculated ambigu-
    ity," seeming at once to be about a rose and a woman.

1951

7   CLARKE, AUSTIN. "Literature in Verse?" Spectator, 187 (23
    November), 714, 716.
        Since Moore is little known here, though well known in
    the United States, it is regrettable that her Collected Po-
    ems lacks an explanatory foreword. Her poetry seems still
    faithful to Imagism. It consists of collections of facts
    and a bit of fancy, sounds at times like a guide-book, ech-
    oes with off-accent rhymes, puts function words in prominent
    places and rhymes them, and gives notes for sources.

8   COFFMAN, STANLEY K., Jr. Imagism: A Chapter for the History
    of Modern Poetry. Norman: University of Oklahoma Press,
    pp. 29, 34, 221, 222-23.
        Not closely associated with Imagism, Moore nevertheless
    found it useful, especially its attention to detail and its
    "making the object real."

9   JARRELL, RANDALL. "The Humble Animal." In The Kenyon Critics:
    Studies in Modern Literature from the Kenyon Review. Edited
    by John Crowe Ransom. Cleveland and New York: The World
    Publishing Co., pp. 277-80.
        Reprint of 1942.4.

10 SERGEANT, HOWARD. "Imagism: An Anglo-American Movement." In
    his Tradition in the Making of Modern Poetry. London:
    Britannicus Liber Ltd., I, 93, 105-07.
        Moore is most the imagist in her "studies of the animal
    world." In observation and phrasing, she captures the thing
    she describes. She is affiliated with John Crowe Ransom in
    "the modulation of her speech rhythms."

11 SMITH, PETER DUVAL. "To Please Herself." The New Stateman and
    Nation, 42 (1 December), 644.
        Moore's poetry, gathered in Collected Poems, praises the
    "tactful virtues." "Critics and Connoisseurs," perhaps her
    best poem, does so, but it also suggests the poet's pride
    in her craft. The better poems are "poems of knowledge";
    others, less successful because of their wordy discursive-
    ness, are "poems about knowledge." The "fear of disliking
    literature" appears throughout her poems. Selected Poems
    was successful because of "the very original subject matter."
    In more recent poems, tact has led to "an impoverishment of
    subject matter that shows itself in a series of violences
    to the ear."

12   STEVENS, WALLACE. "About One of Marianne Moore's Poems." In
     his The Necessary Angel: Essays on Reality and the Imagina-
     tion. New York: Alfred A Knopf, pp. 92-103.
     Reprint of 1948.13.

13   WILLIAMS, WILLIAM CARLOS. The Autobiography of William Carlos
     Williams. New York: Random House, pp. 52, 146, 152, 163-64,
     171, 175, 177, 319.
     I never met Moore at Bryn Mawr, though I did meet Hilda
     Doolittle there. In the years just before the "catastrophe"
     of The Waste Land, Moore was "our saint." Rumor had it that
     Scofield Thayer had proposed to Moore. She is now trans-
     lating the fables of La Fontaine.

1952

1   ADAMS, J. DONALD. "Speaking of Books." The New York Times,
    10 February, sec. 7, p. 2.
    Moore has won the National Book Award for Collected Poems.

2   ALLENTUCK, MARCIA EPSTEIN. "Moore's 'In Distrust of Merits.'"
    The Explicator, 10 (April), item 42.
    The key to "In Distrust of Merits" is its ironic title.

3   ANON. "Bollingen Prize." Publishers' Weekly, 161 (19 January),
    233.
    Moore has been awarded the 1951 Bollingen Prize for her
    Collected Poems. The judges were W. H. Auden (chairman),
    Leonard Bacon, Louise Bogan, Richard Eberhart, and Malcolm
    Cowley.

4   ANON. "Brooklyn 12 Picked for Youth Awards." The New York
    Times, 2 June, p. 18.
    Moore was among twelve people selected to receive the
    annual Youth Oscar awards of Youth United, an agency that
    aids Brooklyn's settlement houses.

5   ANON. "Brooklyn Woman Wins Bollingen Poetry Prize." The New
    York Times, 12 January, p. 16.
    Moore has been awarded the annual Bollingen Prize in Po-
    etry. The $1000 award was made for her Collected Poems.

6   ANON. "College Poets Hold Festival." The New York Times, 5
    April, p. 8.
    Moore and Langston Hughes were guests at a dinner at the
    American Intercollegiate Poetry Reading Festival.

1952

7   ANON. "Jones, Carson, and Moore Win Third National Book Awards."
     Publishers' Weekly, 161 (2 February), 696-97.
         At a reception on 29 January, Moore received the National
     Book Award. The poetry jury included Conrad Aiken, Selden
     Rodman, Winfield T. Scott, Wallace Stevens, and Peter
     Viereck.

8   ANON. "Jones, Miss Carson Get Book Awards...Marianne Moore
     Honored." The New York Times, 30 January, p. 27.
         James Jones, Rachel Carson, and Moore won the third an-
     nual National Book Awards yesterday. It was noted that while
     Jones's From Here to Eternity has sold 250,000 copies and
     Carson's The Sea around Us has sold 180,000, Moore's Collect-
     ed Poems has sold close to 5,000. More said that she was
     surprised it sold one. In her speech, she said that her
     work is called poetry because there is no other category in
     which to put it.

9   ANON. "Marianne (Craig) Moore." Current Biography, 13 (Decem-
     ber), 37-40.
         Biographical sketch and quotations from reviews.
         Reprinted: 1953.4. See also 1968.5.

10   ANON. "Marianne Moore Wins Bollingen Prize." Library Journal,
     77 (15 February), 295.
         Moore has received the Bollingen Prize in Poetry.

11   ANON. "People." Life, 32 (11 February), 37.
         Moore has received a National Book Award for 1951.

12   ANON. Review of Collected Poems. The United States Quarterly
     Book Review, 8 (March), 33-34.
         Moore's poetry is "pedantic detail magically become rich-
     ness, precise moral analysis become wise and humorous con-
     cern, and tough integrity become humane dialectic."

13   ANON. "Sketches of the Pulitzer Prize Winners in Journalism,
     Letters and Music for 1952. Marianne Moore." The New York
     Times, 6 May, p. 24.
         Biographical sketch, including a list of awards.

14   ANON. "Youth Unit Honors 12 at Dinner Here." The New York
     Times, 15 June, p. 29.
         Moore was among those who received Youth Oscars for being
     inspirations to the young people of the eight Brooklyn set-
     tlement houses.

1952

15 BLACKMUR, R. P. "The Method of Marianne Moore." In his <u>Language as Gesture: Essays in Poetry</u>. New York: Harcourt, Brace and Co., pp. 260-85.
    Reprint of 1935.3.

16 BOGAN, LOUISE. "Books-Verse." <u>The New Yorker</u>, 28 (2 August), 65.
    <u>Collected Poems</u> has rightfully been awarded the Pulitzer Prize, Bollingen Prize, and National Book Award. Moore combines the traditional and contemporary.

17 B[REIT], H[ARVEY]. "A Liberator of Poems." <u>The New York Times Book Review</u>, 3 February, p. 10.
    Moore does not write enough. <u>Collected Poems</u> reveals her "intelligence, sensibility and feeling" and her "cool sense ot structure." Perhaps more than any other poet, she has "liberated verse," shown its possibilities, while not giving in to license. Her poems are "carefully made" and concerned with emotion.

18 COLE, THOMAS. "The Revised Poems of Marianne Moore." <u>Imagi</u>, 6, no. 1, [pp. 11-12].
    <u>Collected Poems</u> has revised versions of many poems.

19 DEUTSCH, BABETTE. <u>Poetry in Our Time</u>. New York: Henry Holt and Co., pp. 92-93, 95, 211-12, 246, 377.
    Moore's "observations extend to the ethical realm." Elizabeth Bishop "is one of her literary descendants." Moore's use of quotations sometimes makes her work "a bibliographical curiosity."
    Excerpted: 1974.2.

20 ENGLE, PAUL. "Miss Moore Keeps to Narrow Path in Her Superb Poetry." <u>Chicago Sunday Tribune Magazine of Books</u>, 20 January, p. 5.
    Moore persists in writing her unique kind of poetry, which is "crammed with the world's forms of life and things."

21 FOWLIE, WALLACE. "Marianne Moore." <u>The Sewanee Review</u>, 60 (July-September), 537-47.
    The study of a major poet such as Moore raises questions about the power of poetry. One current theory, that poetry creates a world, seems especially to apply to Moore. Her poetry, with its incorporated objects, seems to reflect art become substance. To read her work is to read a "construction." Yet her work reflects as well a mystical acceptance of the world. The poems are creations of her intellect,

1952

itself informed by emotion and arcanic experience. She uses
language to capture that which is outside it.

22   HOFFMAN, DAN G. "Moore's 'See in the Midst of Fair Leaves.'"
     The Explicator, 10 (March), item 34.
          "See in the Midst of Fair Leaves," read in the light of
     its source in Daniel 6:12-22, has as its theme "the indivis-
     ibility of angel, man, and monster." It "attributes the
     fall of man to selfhood."

23   HONIG, EDWIN. "Three Master." Voices, no. 148 (May-August),
     pp. 35-37.
          Moore's poems in Collected Poems are like museums "in
     which the questions of imagination and reality are tran-
     scended by the highest criterion of taste and a mastery of
     poetic artifice."

24   HUMPHRIES, ROLFE. "Verse Chronicle." The Nation, 174 (2 Feb-
     ruary), 113.
          Collected Poems contains animals, artifacts, and quota-
     tions presented with wit, craft, and feeling.

25   JARRELL, RANDALL. "Thoughts about Marianne Moore." Partisan
     Review, 19 (November-December), 687-700.
          One now hears from English reviewers of Collected Poems
     what was once often heard in America--that Moore is no poet.
     In America she now wins prizes and receives much praise,
     though until recently she was little read. She is unjustly
     treated as "a sort of museum poet." She is a poet of par-
     ticulars but also of perception and moral abstraction. She
     discovers poetry in the world. Her recent poetry tends to
     be less abstract, less remore, less "armoured."
          Reprinted: 1953.12. Portions reprinted: 1963.9,
     1964.17, 1969.14, 1969.28.

26   McDONALD, GERALD D. Brief notice of Collected Poems. Library
     Journal, 77 (15 March), 533.
          Collected Poems is "the outstanding poetry book of the
     season."

27   RODMAN, SELDEN. "Miracle of Integrity and Wit." New York
     Herald Tribune Book Review, 28 (27 January), 3.
          A poem reviewing Collected Poems. Moore's use of allu-
     sion sometimes tires. The source of her method is obscure,
     though Browning, Hopkins, and Whitman are involved. The
     best poem in the collection is "A Grave." More makes real
     "a world of artifice and elegance."

28 ROSENTHAL, M. L. "Jubal, Jabal and Moore." The New Republic,
      126 (7 April), 21.
        Moore's poetry is more serious than those who cannot see
      past her wit realize.

*29 SAWYER, KENNETH B., Jr. "Praises and Crutches." Hopkins Re-
      view, 5, no. 4, 126-32.
        Listed in Sheehy and Lohf (1958.17), p. 31.

30 S[MITH], H[ARRISON]. "The Bollingen Prize." The Saturday Re-
      view, 35 (2 February), 23.
        Moore has been awarded the Bollingen Prize. Her verse
      is individual and compact. Moore is a "skilled craftsman"
      whose work "is distinguished by her use of telling metaphors
      and restrained control of an ardent imagination and strong
      emtions." Includes biographical sketch.

31 VAZAKAS, BYRON. "Three Modern Old Masters: Moore-Stevens-
      Williams." New Mexico Quarterly, 22 (Winter), 431-34.
        Moore's Collected Poems shows her "persistent originali-
      ty." Hers is not a poetry, in John Crowe Ransom's words,
      of "primitive or heroic occasions." But it is genuine. Her
      heroism or greatness resides not in the magnitude of her
      subjects but in her oracular collations of curiosa.

1953

1   ANDERSON, MARGARET. Editorial comment. In her The Little Re-
      view Anthology. New York: Hermitage House, pp. 187-88.
        I do not like Moore's "You Say You Said." Pound and I
      disagreed about Moore. I do not like "intellectual poetry."
      While Eliot "uses his mind to reveal the life of his emo-
      tions," Moore "uses the life of her mind as her subject
      matter." Poets are concerned with the "noumenal world";
      Moore with the phenomenal.

2   ANON. "Eisenhower Lauds L.I.U. Fight on Bias." The New York
      Times, 12 June, p. 18.
        Moore was honored at Long Island University's commencement.

3   ANON. "Life Goes on a Zoo Tour with a Famous Poet." Life, 35
      (21 September), 202-204.
        Moore loves animals and has lived in Brooklyn for twenty-
      five years.

1953

4   ANON. "Marianne (Craig) Moore." <u>Current Biography: Who's</u>
     <u>News and Why, 1952</u>. New York: The H. W. Wilson Co., pp.
     435-37.
          Reprint of 1952.9.

5   ANON. "Much Honored Poet Wins National Institute Prize." <u>The</u>
     <u>New York Times</u>, 17 April, p. 16.
          Moore has been awarded the National Institute of Arts
     and Letters' gold medal for poetry. Glenway Wescott will
     present her with the medal in a ceremony next month.

6   ANON. "Receives $5,000 Award from Bryn Mawr College." <u>The</u>
     <u>New York Times</u>, 16 May, p. 9.
          Moore was tonight awarded the M. Carey Thomas Award of
     Bryn Mawr College. The prize was established in 1922 and
     has been awarded to six women.

7   ANON. "Winning Woman." <u>Newsweek</u>, 42 (28 December), 40.
          The <u>Woman's Home Companion</u> has selected Moore one of the
     six most successful women of the year.

8   ANON. "Wright Honored, Voices Humility. Institute of Arts
     and Letters Awards Medals to Architect and Marianne Craig
     Moore." <u>The New York Times</u>, 28 May, p. 28.
          Moore was today presented with the Institute's gold
     medal.

9   BOGAN, LOUISE. "Reading Contemporary Poetry." <u>College English</u>,
     14 (February), 255-60.
          Moore's poetry is typical of contemporary poetry in its
     freedom without formlessness, its indirectness of statement,
     and its subtlely presented emotion. The poem "The Steeple-
     Jack" has as its theme "safety versus danger" and shows
     Moore's flexible syllabics, emotional reticence, sensitivity
     to language, condensed style, and delight in natural objects.
     Her method is "expository"; her rhythm is that of prose.
     Her drawing conclusions from particulars reminds one of La
     Fontaine. Her later poetry is less emotionally reticent.

10   HOFFMAN, DANIEL G. "Miss Moore." <u>Antioch Review</u>, 12 (March),
     123-25.
          Like Whitman, Moore has a "democratic inclusiveness."
     But unlike him, she carefully delineates the things she
     includes. She captures the actual and relates it to the
     spiritual forces of "love, courage, humility, integrity,
     and joy." Like the steeple-jack in the poem of that title,
     she sees the world to transcend it.

1954

11 HOFFMAN, FREDERICK J. "Marianne Moore: Imaginary Gardens and
    Real Toads." Poetry, 83 (December), 152-57.
        Of those who met in Alfred Kreymborg's home in the days
    of Others (1915-1919), Moore was the "'moralist,' and witty
    rational commentator." She is a poet of acute observation.
    She is a "literalist of the imagination," as she says (in
    Yeats's words) in "Poetry."

12 JARRELL, RANDALL. "Her Shield." In his Poetry and the Age.
    New York: Alfred A Knopf, pp. 185-207.
        Reprint of 1952.25.

13 _____. "The Humble Animal." In his Poetry and the Age. New
    York: Alfred A Knopf, pp. 179-84.
        Reprint of 1942.4.

14 LEGLER, PHILIP FERGUSON. "Marianne Moore and the Idea of Free-
    dom." Poetry, 83 (December), 158-67.
        An analysis of "The Jerboa" will reveal the nature of the
    whole body of work in Collected Poems. The poem is "a se-
    ries of tensions and anticlimaxes" and "dramatic and ironic
    contrasts." The theme of the poem is the attainment of
    freedom thorough the realization of one's limitations.

15 MARITAIN, JACQUES. Creative Intuition in Art and Poetry: The
    A. W. Mellon Lectures in the Fine Arts. Bollingen Series
    XXXV.I. New York: Pantheon Books, p. 249n.
        It may be that poets like Moore fear "the subjectivity
    of their poetic experience" and thus create "an almost
    purely visual or perceptual poetry."

16 POUND, EZRA. "Marianne Moore and Mina Loy." In The Little
    Review Anthology. Edited by Margaret Anderson. New York:
    Hermitage House, pp. 187-88.
        Reprint of 1918.3.

                            1954

1   ANON. Brief notice of The Fables of La Fontaine. The Booklist,
    50 (1 July), 415.
        Moore's translations, faithful to the original, "should
    attract even the reader who does not make the reading of
    poetry a habitual enterprise."

2   ANON. "New Shine on Old Truths." Time, 63 (24 May), 108.
        Moore has published only three poems since 1945 [sic].
    She has been at work translating La Fontaine's fables,

                            43

1954

which she has now completed. Her translations are superior
to those of "the standard translators." She attempted to
capture La Fontaine's literal meaning and delicate rhymes.
She had had "only three years of school French," and her
first efforts had to be discarded.

3   ANON. "A Selected List of Children's Books." The Commonweal,
      61 (19 November), 200.
         Along with Shakespeare's plays, La Fontaine's fables
      should be "in every American household." Moore's transla-
      tion is good.

4   BOGAN, LOUISE. "Books: Verse." The New Yorker, 30 (4 Sep-
      tember), 75.
         In rendering La Fontaine's fables into modern English,
      Moore has captured their form and tone. Moore's own poems
      resemble his in style, humor, and intelligence.
         Reprinted: 1955.10, 1970.4.

5   CANNELL, KATHLEEN. "Garden with Real Toads." The Christian
      Science Monitor, Atlantic edition, 1 July, p. 11.
         Moore's translations of La Fontaine's fables capture
      their sense and essence. They are "a poetic recreation" of
      the original.

6   CIARDI, JOHN. "Strictness and Faithfulness." The Nation, 178
      (19 June), 525.
         In translating La Fontaine's fables, Moore has attempted
      to follow Pound's superb but impossible theory of repro-
      ducing rhythm and rhyme while maintaining natural word
      order. In her most successful translations--for example,
      "Bitch and Friend" and "The Dog Who Dropped Substance for
      Shadow"--she forsakes Poundian strictness for a more sen-
      sible faithfulness to the experience of the poem.

7   COLUM, MARY M. "France's Only Epic." The Saturday Review, 37
      (24 July), 16.
         Moore's translation of La Fontaine's fables is "a note-
      worthy achievement," especially given her limited knowledge
      of French. Moore mistakenly attempts to capture the meter
      of original and fails to capture La Fontaine's naturalness.

8   ESSEKS, ALBERT W. "Fables of La Fontaine." Reader, 1 (Janu-
      ary), 63.
         Moore's translations are excellent. One hears her voice
      in them.

1954

9   FOWLIE, WALLACE. "The American Word for La Fontaine." The
    New York Times Book Review, 16 May, pp. 1, 3.
        In perhaps the most extensive undertaking of its kind by
    an American poet, Moore has translated all 241 of La
    Fontaine's fables. Little known outside France except as
    a poet for children, La Fontaine is a classical writer whose
    work, like Moore's, combines "heart and mind." As their
    "outstanding technical achievement," the translations have
    a "recasting of the complex interplay of rhyme." The dif-
    ficulty she successfully overcame was that of finding "com-
    mon American speech for the common speech of France" while
    retaining La Fontaine's elegance. The fables are signifi-
    cant more for their art than for their meaning or moral
    lessons.

10 G[LAUBER], R[OBERT] H. "Opinion." The Beloit Poetry Journal,
    5 (Winter), 27-28.
        Moore's translations of La Fontaine's fables are a fine
    combination of two poets.

11 GUTHRIE, RAMON. "A Rendering of La Fontaine." New York Her-
    ald Tribune Book Review, 30 (4 July), 7.
        Moore's translations of the fables get La Fontaine into
    English and follow his rhyme and rhythm as closely as pos-
    sible, but they are not "an equivalent of La Fontaine."
    In following his form, Moore loses his content, though pre-
    serving some of his spontaneity.

12 HUTCHENS, JOHN K. "Lady of the Fables." New York Herald Tri-
    bune Book Review, 30 (13 June), 2.
        Upon publication of her translation of the fables, Moore
    says that she knows little French, had not read La Fontaine
    before she started, began translating (in 1945) at the sug-
    gestion of W. H. Auden, did poorly in French at Bryn Mawr,
    could not make herself understood in France in 1911, mis-
    read accent marks, went through about twenty drafts of each
    fable, and believes La Fontaine to be forthright but moral.

13 JACOBSON, MAX L. "To the Editor." New York Times Book Review,
    27 June, p. 26.
        Fowlie (1954.9) is incorrect when he speaks of Moore's
    fidelity to La Fontaine's French. La Fontaine's "delight-
    ful expressions and little jokes" and his music have been
    lost in her translations.

14 JOOST, NICHOLAS. "The Double Richness of Two Distinguished
    Talents." The Commonweal, 60 (23 July), 395-96.

1954

        Moore's translation of La Fontaine's fables brings to-
gether "the greatest fabulist of modern times and the finest
woman poet now writing in English." For the first time, the
fables have a translation that approximates "their Gallic
charm." The success is in part the result of advice Moore
received from her family and from Harry Levin, Malcolm
Cowley, Pascal Covici, and Monroe Engel and of the influence
of Pound's principle of translation. Moore's work was not
a waste of ten years. It puts her "in the company of Bede,
Alfred, Chaucer, Florio, Chapman, and Dryden."

15   ____. "Exploring La Fontaine's World." Chicago Sunday Tribune Magazine of Books, 6 June, p. 6.
        Moore's translation of La Fontaine's fables "recreates"
his work. Her success comes from her "amused and sympathetic preoccupation" with animals and people.

16   KENNER, HUGH. "Supreme in Her Abnormality." Poetry, 84 (September), 356-63.
        In her translations of La Fontaine's fables, Moore has
discovered a suitable and natural idiom that recreates civilized but not slick speech. While La Fontaine's "curiously
pastoral urbanity" has misled other translators into making
his poems into simplistic maxims, Moore "complicates the
diction" to assure that the reader understands. There are
lapses from the French, but on the whole the translation
"succeeds astonishingly."
        Reprinted: 1958.19, 1969.28.

17   KICKI, W. J. "To the Editor." New York Times Book Review, 27
June, p. 26.
        Fowlie's assertion (1954.9) that La Fontaine is "virtu-
ally unknown outside of France" is questionable.

18   LANGLAND, JOHN. "To the Editor." New York Times Book Review,
27 June, p. 26.
        Donald Sutherland's translations of four of La Fontaine's
fables are superior to Moore's excellent, precise, and
"sometimes chilling" versions. A response to 1954.9.

19   McDONALD, GERALD D. Brief notice of the Fables of La Fontaine.
Library Journal, 79 (15 June), 1232.
        Moore's translations preserve La Fontaine's satire and
sophistication but embody "something of her own wit and tone
of voice."

20   MIZENER, ARTHUR. "Transformations." The Kenyon Review, 16
(Summer), 473-79.

Moore's translations of the fables of La Fontaine are
"very bad." In hindsight it is possible to see two reasons
why Moore should be unsuited for the task of translation
that Auden first suggested to her: she has little interest
in narrative, and she tends "to make people inferior to animals," to prefer the natural to the civilized. For what-
ever reason, almost all of the translations contain "mud-
dles." They are sometimes too literal, more often not
literal enough. They are often garbled in syntax and
"undistinguished" in rhythm.

21 NEMEROV, HOWARD. "A Few Bricks from Babel." The Sewanee Re-
    view, 62 (October-December), 655-59.
        Moore's translations of La Fontaine's fables are "terri-
    ble." Despite her fondness for animals, Moore is no fabu-
    list. In her own poetry, she uses animals not to act out
    "her moralities" but "to provide a minutely detailed, finely
    perceived symbolic knot to be a center for the pattern of
    her recondite meditations." One source of her failure is
    her "uncertainty about the ideal degree of her dependence
    on the French: as poems to be read in English, they are
    irritatingly awkward, elliptical, complicated, and very
    jittery as to the meter; as renderings of the French they
    vacillate between pedantic strictness and strange liberty."
        Reprinted: 1963.15, 1969.28. Excerpted: 1975.2.

22 NICHOLS, LEWIS. "Talk with Marianne Moore." The New York
    Times Book Review, 16 May, p. 30.
        According to Moore, she began translating La Fontaine at
    the suggestion of Auden in 1945, worked full-time on them,
    received guidance from Harry Levin, and wrote four complete
    drafts. Her favorite fables are "The Dog Who Dropped Sub-
    stance for Shadow" and "Bitch and Friend." The worst is
    "Middle Age and Two Possible Wives." The most difficult to
    translate was "An Animal in the Moon." Moore does not think
    La Fontaine indelicate.

23 POORE, CHARLES. "Books of the Times. The New York Times, 20
    May, p. 29.
        Moore's translations of La Fontaine's fables are lucid
    and will give the fables "an American immortality."

24 SNODGRASS, W. D. "Elegance in Marianne Moore." The Western
    Review, 19 (Autumn), 57-64.
        Moore's earlier poems (e.g., "To a Snail," "Peter," and
    "The Hero") have "a conversational tone livened only by
    brisk juxtapositions" of images achieved through "syntactic
    cunning." But later poems (e.g., "He 'Digesteth Harde Yron'"

1954

and "A Carriage from Sweden") have an increased musicality
created by patterns of internal rhyme and echoes of an
accentual-syllabic meter embodied in her syllabic (and
therefore nonrhythmic) prosody. Musical scansions of "No
Swan So Fine," "His Shield," and "Propriety" reveal her use
of rhythmic patterns that, while not always obvious, "echo
throughout...and deeply affect our apprehension of the
poems."

25 SOUTHWORTH, JAMES G. "Marianne Moore." In his <u>More Modern
American Poets</u>. New York: Macmillan, pp. 41-48.
    In reprinting her poems, Moore has deleted those "in
which her personal feelings interfered with her objectivity
as an artist." Her objectivity, however, does not preclude
emotion. About love she has little to say. She writes
about animals. She uses alliteration to heighten her vivid
descriptions. Her rhythms have become less prose-like,
more patterned. Beneath the surface of description are
general observations.

26 TATE, ALLEN. "Marianne Moore." In his <u>Sixty American Poets,
1896-1944</u>. Revised edition. Washington, D. C.: Library
of Congress, pp. 89-91.
    Moore "will never be popular" because of her syllabic
meter, "intellectualism," and "severity." Includes brief
bibliography.

27 UNTERMEYER, LOUIS. "Poets without Readers: The Sad State of
Poetry in the United States." <u>Américas</u>, 6 (September), 26.
    Moore is "the most distinguished of present-day women
poets." Her poems combine wit and imagination. "There are
those who claim that Miss Moore makes a witty kind of mon-
tage of things seen and things recalled, that hers is not
so much poetry as a kind of rhythmical geometry."

28 WENDT, VIOLA. "On Reading Marianne Moore." <u>The Beloit Poetry
Journal</u>, 4 (Summer), 18-19.
    Poem.

29 WESCOTT, GLENWAY. "Presentation to Marianne Craig Moore of
the Gold Medal for Poetry." <u>Proceedings of the American
Academy of Arts and Letters</u>, Second Series, no. 4, pp. 11-13.
    My admiration for Moore has grown over the years. Now
honored, she worked for decades with little "ease or profit
or popularity." Although she has "perhaps the most poetical
personality on earth now," she writes in a "relatively pro-
saic style." Her poetry "gathers and preserves" objects on

which she philosophizes and moralizes. With her, despite
the confusion around us, poetry endures.

30   WILLIAMS, WILLIAM CARLOS. <u>Selected Essays of William Carlos
     Williams</u>. New York: Random House, pp. 121-31, 292-94.
     Reprints of 1925.20 and 1948.16.

1955

1   ANON. "Academy of Arts Adds 6 Members." <u>The New York Times</u>,
    10 December, p. 43.
        It was announced yesterday that Moore was elected to the
    American Academy of Arts and Letters.

2   ANON. Brief notice of <u>Predilections</u>. <u>The Booklist</u>, 51 (1
    June), 407.
        Moore's essays are "as private, disciplined, and com-
    pressed as poetry."

3   ANON. "Moore, Marianne Craig." In <u>Twentieth Century Authors:
    A Biographical Dictionary of Modern Literature</u>. First Sup-
    plement. Edited by Stanley J. Kunitz and Vineta Colby.
    New York: The H. W. Wilson Co., pp. 684-85.
        Corrects some biographical information in the earlier
    sketch (1942.1). Says that Moore is a poet of craft and
    life and that response to her poetry has been "almost uni-
    formly favorable."

4   ANON. Review of <u>Predilections</u>. <u>The United States Quarterly
    Book Review</u>, 11 (September), 344-45.
        In the twenty-three essays and reviews in <u>Predilections</u>,
    Moore is like "the attentive reader or beholder," allowing
    no abstractions to intervene. The essays make much use of
    quotation.

5   ANON. "Warning on Conformity." <u>The New York Times</u>, 9 June,
    p. 22.
        Moore was awarded an honorary Doctor of Letters degree
    by Douglas College.

6   ARROWSMITH, WILLIAM. "All about Ripeness." <u>The Hudson Review</u>,
    8 (Autumn), 443-45.
        Moore's criticism gathered in <u>Predilections</u> expresses
    her gratitude for art that contains "precision of feeling."
    When she finds fault, she does so with tact of the same
    sort that accounts for the difficulty of her poetry. It

1955

alters "the familiar relation between perceiver and object."
Moore imposes humility on herself and her objects.

7   ASBURG, EDITH EVANS. "End Conformity, Stevenson Urges." The
    New York Times, 7 June, p. 36.
        Moore was among seven women given honorary degrees by
    Smith College.

8   BARRETT, WILLIAM. "Reading over a Poet's Shoulder." The Sat-
    urday Review, 38 (21 May), 14.
        In her poetry and prose, Moore lets objects speak for
    themselves. The essays in Predilections provide readers
    the opportunity to read along with Moore. The best essays
    deal with fellow poets.

9   BOGAN, LOUISE. "Books: Verse." The New Yorker, 31 (30 July),
    67.
        The essays in Predilections gather information, trans-
    late it into facts, and fit the facts into patterns.

10 _____. Selected Criticism: Prose, Poetry. New York: The
    Noonday Press, pp. 252-57, 377-80.
        Reprints of 1944.4, 1954.4.

11 BORDEN, ARTHUR R., Jr. Review of Predilections. Shenandoah,
    7 (Autumn), 86-87.
        The criteria Moore uses in her essays are "humility, con-
    centration, and gusto." Although the impressionistic essays
    are good, readers will be interested primarily in Moore
    herself.

12 CANNELL, KATHLEEN. "With Precision, Gusto, and Sense of Won-
    der." The Christian Science Monitor, Atlantic edition, 2
    June, p. 15.
        Moore's delightful, precise, Jamesian conversation--in-
    deed, a sort of conversation between Moore and James--can
    be found in Predilections. Moore is reassuringly moral,
    unlike many modern novelists but like Eliot, Stevens, and
    Auden.

13 CLUBB, O. EDMUND. "Criticism by Quotation." The Nation, 181
    (9 July), 29.
        In Predilections, Moore makes the pastiche "into a pe-
    culiarly effective tool."

14 DEUTSCH, BABETTE. "Reticent Candor of a Poet." New York
    Herald Tribune Book Review, 31 July, p. 6.

In poetry and prose, Moore is a "mosaicist." Portions
of Predilections seem to come from "a writer's commonplace
book." Sometimes, especially in the more general essays,
one could wish for less reticence and quotation and more
perception.

15 ENGLE, PAUL. "A Poet Turns to Prose." Chicago Sunday Tribune
    Magazine of Books, 5 June, p. 5.
        Predilections shows that Moore, as the dust jacket says,
    is "a poet's best reader."

16 GABLE, SISTER MARIELLA. Review of Predilections. The Ameri-
    can Benedictine Review, 6 (Winter), 458-59.
        Moore, "one of America's excellent minor poets," writes
    essays with "astringent distinction."

17 HOFFMAN, FREDERICK J. "Some 'Imaginary Gardens with Real Toads
    in Them.'" In his The Twenties: American Writing in the
    Postwar Decade. New York: The Viking Press, pp. 175,
    176-79. 186.
        Moore observes and comments. In her, a "vivid pictorial
    sense" unites "with a conversational shrewdness." Her
    "Poetry" is in esthetics and a defense of poetry as a place
    where objects "assume a new reality."

18 HONIG, EDWIN. "Reading Miss Moore's La Fontaine." New Mexico
    Quarterly, 25 (Summer), 249.
        Poem.

19 HOWE, IRVING. "The Greenest Land She's Almost Seen." The New
    Republic, 132 (23 May), 20.
        The critical essays in Predilections are curious, uncon-
    ventional. Moore's style is elliptical and imagistic--so
    given to particulars that it approaches obscurity. Moore
    seems intent on sounding the way one would imagine her to
    sound in prose. But the essays have some fine insights.

20 JARRELL, RANDALL. "A Matter of Opinion." The New York Times
    Book Review, 29 May, p. 5.
        The essays in Predilections are appreciative rather than
    critical. She does not discuss what she disapproves of--or,
    if she does, she merely suggests her dislike imaginatively,
    perhaps through aphorism, as she does with Jean Cocteau's
    "Infernal Machine." There are poems in her prose. She is
    especially good in writing about Stevens, Williams, Pound,
    James, and the writer's craft.

51

1955

21 KALB, BERNARD. Biographical sketch. The Saturday Review, 38
      (21 May), 14.
         Moore's poetry has won her every major poetry award.
      Recently she said that she has never been quoted precisely.
      Her Brooklyn apartment is crowded with books and mementos.
      She says that she has never referred to herself as a poet.

22 LATTIMORE, RICHMOND. "Parnassus Is a Rugged Mountain." The
      Hudson Review, 7 (Winter), 632-34.
         Despite some obscurity, Moore's translations of La
      Fontaine's fables are "an enormous job impressively done."
      Moore has recreated in English "the whole metrical scheme,
      that is line length and placing of rhymes, in each Fable."

23 McDONALD, GERALD D. Brief notice of Predilections. Library
      Journal, 80 (July), 1592.
         Moore's essays employ much quotation but remain hers.
      Predilections is for college or large public libraries.

24 MILLER, MARY OWINGS. "Miss Moore Is Herself." Voices, no.
      158 (September-December), pp. 35.
         Poem.

25 MUIR, EDWIN. "Thou Art Translated." The Observer (London),
      24 April, p. 14.
         Moore's translation of La Fontaine has produced "a vol-
      ume of fables by Marianne Moore," a fine addition to her
      poetry and an "indirect commentary on the poetry of La
      Fontaine."

26 O'GORMAN, NED. "The Poet As Critic." The Commonweal, 62 (17
      June), 284-85.
         Moore writes criticism "with the mind of a critic" but
      with "the language of poetry."

1956

1   AMIS, KINGSLEY. "Divagations." Spectator, 196 (20 April), 552.
         The essays in Predilections lack "any sense of relevance
      or direction." They are overblown or fuzzy statements or
      are serial jottings from Moore's reading.

2   ANON. "Authors Guild Elects 11." The New York Times, 12 De-
      cember, p. 36.
         At its annual meeting yesterday, the Authors Guild
      elected eleven people, including Moore, to serve on its
      council.

1956

3   ANON. Brief notice of <u>Like a Bulwark</u>. <u>The Booklist and Sub-</u>
       <u>scription Books Bulletin,</u> 53 (1 November), 114.
            In <u>Like a Bulwark</u>, the notes "are almost as significant
       as the lyrics themselves."

4   ANON. "Native American Culture." <u>The Commonweal</u>, 65 (19 No-
       vember), 62.
            Americans have reacted to the European critics' charges
       of American "cultural immaturity" by retreating to the lit-
       tle magazines or by claiming that the engineer is the Amer-
       ican artist. What Americans needed "was just one piece of
       concrete evidence to show that culture could flourish on
       native American soil." And now we have it: Moore's "An
       Ode to the Brooklyn Dodgers" ["Hometown Piece for Messrs.
       Alston and Reese"]. The form is not derivative; the rhythm
       captures the march of the crippled, aging "Bums" to the
       National League pennant; and the subject is "as indigenously
       American as apple pie or teachers' colleges."

5   ANON. "The Poet as Critic." <u>The Times Literary Supplement</u>,
       no. 2,818 (2 March), p. 135.
            Moore's <u>Predilections</u> is representative of the "marginal,
       subjective, spectacular criticism" being written by a number
       of American poets--for example, Cummings, Williams, and
       Stevens. It is marked by overdependence on quotation and
       lack of "plain statement." <u>Predilections</u> is interesting
       for the light it sheds on Moore, not on her subjects.

6   ANON. "Two Arts Groups Make 24 Awards." <u>The New York Times</u>,
       24 May, p. 25.
            Moore was inducted into the American Academy yesterday.

7   BORROFF, MARIE. "'Tom Fool at Jamaica' by Marianne Moore:
       Meaning and Structure." <u>College English</u>, 17 (May), 466-69.
            The theme of "Tom Fool at Jamaica" is "a kind of moral
       excellence underlying superiority of action or performance."
       The abstract theme is not presented abstractly but embodied
       in the particulars of the poem. The poem presents "the
       experience of reflection," not the product of it. The poem
       is emotionally dynamic, building to "a crescendo of inten-
       sity" in the fourth stanza.

8   BRUMBAUGH, THOMAS B. "Concerning Miss Moore's Museum."
       <u>Twentieth Century Literature</u>, 1 (January), 191-95.
            Moore's "demand for sympathy and rightness in artistic
       truth" implied in "Poetry" and stated in "When I Buy Pic-
       tures" is similar to the test for painting established by
       sixth-century Chinese artists. Her fondness for Chinese

53

1956

art objects and even Dürer's drawings (see "The Steeple-
Jack") is based on their implosivity, their possession of
a "spiritual rhythm" beneath their "technically superb surfaces." Moore's translation of Stifter's Rock Crystal and
the comparison of her notebooks (in Tiger's Eye, October
1947) with Stifter's reveal the similarity in their "conscious fastidiousness," interest in visual detail, and
"infatuation with the gemütlich." Moore is a scholar-
collector. Her art objects in What Are Years and Nevertheless serve "a slightly more outgoing and didactic purpose
in the earlier poems."

9   BURKE, KENNETH. "Likings of an Observationist." Poetry, 87
     (January), 239-47.
         Predilections is "splendid," useful (by way of admonition
     and example) as "a study in stylistic scruples." In striv-
     ing for precision, Moore sacrifices continuity and avoids
     treating parts of a work that do not lend themselves to her
     aphoristic or miniaturistic methods, as in her essay on
     Henry James. Her essays on Williams, Cummings, Eliot, and
     Louise Bogan are "fine acts of identification"--momentary
     and partial glimpses of them. Her essay on the Dial "twits"
     one of my titles and too generously lists me as a managing
     editor. Her predilections for certain writers and other
     figures reflect her own traits. Pavlova, for example, seems
     to have represented perfectly Moore's ideals of discipline,
     remoteness, and non-mysterious spirituality. In both deduc-
     tive and inductive essays, Moore generalizes no further than
     her particulars allow. In "Feeling and Precision" she es-
     tablishes a duality in which the term moral seems to shift
     its application from feeling to precision and back or to
     establish itself in triadic relationship with feeling and
     precision. This confusion reflects "the motivational
     center" of her work, that is, "the fusion whereby one can
     never be quite sure whether her judgments are ethical or
     esthetic." "Humility, Concentration, and Gusto" reveals
     Moore's view of humility as an intellectual or technical
     virtue. Throughout the book, Moore's concerns are the co-
     existence of restraint and precision, the art of understate-
     ment, the "dignity and responsibility of her calling,"
     inversions of antecedent-consequent relationships, puns,
     idiosyncrasy, and nice distinctions.
         Reprinted: 1969.28.

10   CORKE, HILARY. "Essence of Criticism." The Listener, 55 (12
     April), 423.

Predilections is a collection of prose as concentrated as Moore's verse. The prose is gnomic, leaving the reader the task of perceiving the connections between statements.

11 DAVIE, DONALD. "Economiastick Criticism." The New Statesman and Nation, 51 (3 March), 190.
    In Predilections Moore is "one of the cheer-leaders of literature." Some of the reviews "are very slight indeed." The pieces on Stevens are good. Her essays are her brand of poetic prose, which happens to be "undigestible." Gaps in logic that work in poetry irritate and mislead in prose. Moore is a good poet, but she needs to be more considerate of her reader in her prose.

12 KENNEBECK, EDWIN. "Critics' Choices for Christmas." The Commonweal, 65 (7 December), 259.
    The poems in Like a Bulwark are beautiful, eccentric, and precise.

13 M. F. C. "Oblique Critic." Manchester Guardian, 7 February, p. 4.
    Predilections records Moore's "random observations" about her likes. Her prose is not entirely happy.

14 MADDOCKS, MELVIN. "Eliot and Miss Moore." The Christian Science Monitor, Atlantic edition, 25 October, p. 5.
    In Like a Bulwark, Moore has turned to American experience rather than to European literature for "her sources of inspiration." Still, like Eliot's, her poetry is "academic." The poems in Like a Bulwark do not pretend to be great verse.

15 POORE, CHARLES. "Books of the Times." The New York Times, 4 December, p. 37.
    Like a Bulwark is perhaps Moore's finest book.

16 REES, RALPH. "The Imagery of Marianne Moore." Ph.D. dissertation, Pennsylvania State University, 158 pp. Abstracted in Dissertation Abstracts, 17 (1957), 366.
    Moore's imagery and precision reflect her interest in that which "individualizes," or "armors," and in ideas that unify the things of the world. Despite the concreteness of her often startling images, Moore is interested not in the thing itself but in the idea of the thing as discovered by the imagination. She uses irony and humor to counter a tendency toward didacticism.

1956

17 RICHART, BETTE. "In the Grand Tradition." The Commonweal, 65
    (28 December), 338-39.
        Moore's poetry combines "compassion and precision" and
    contains a "commonplace ethic redeemed by rare learning."
    Moore is eccentric but not merely eccentric.
    Excerpted: 1960.17.

18 ROSENBERG, FRANCIS COLEMAN. "'A Refusal to Be False.'"
    Voices, no. 160 (May-August), pp. 39-41.
        Predilections is a record of Moore's "preferences and
    predispositions and predilections."

19 SAX, WENDALL. "Marianne Moore at NYU: 'Egomania Is Not a
    Duty.'" The Village Voice, 12 December, p. 3.
        At the NYU English Graduate Association, Moore spoke on
    "Poetry--What Should We Ask of It?" She said that the
    writing and reading of poetry should be enjoyable and that
    poetry should contain human values. After the lecture, she
    talked about her days in Greenwich Village.

20 SPENDER, STEPHEN. "Book Reviews." The London Magazine, 3
    (June), 73-75.
        The value of Moore's essays in Predilections may lie less
    in what they say about the writing of others than in Moore's
    own demonstration of "the most delicate mechanism of writ-
    ing." She does not, in fact, say much: her essays are col-
    lections of statements and quotations with an associative
    rather than logical order. Moore's renderings of La
    Fontaine's fables in Selected Fables make use of her gift
    for observation, "feeling for animals, and...lively sense
    of narrative" but fail to capture the rhythm of the French.

21 TOYNBEE, PHILIP. "The Prose of a Poetess." The Observer
    (London), 29 January, p. 9.
        Moore's prose in Predilections is "remarkable." If it
    is sometimes private, it also aims for precision and
    felicity.

22 WILBUR, RICHARD. "The Heart of the Thing." The New York
    Times Book Review, 11 November, p. 18.
        In seven of the eleven poems in Like a Bulwark, "Moore
    performs her peculiar miracle, which consists of exacting
    the beautiful from the good." Her imagination "combines
    morality and preciosity." The morals of her poems are
    central; the preciosity is exuberance, not ornament.

1957

1 ANON. "Ars Poetica." Time, 69 (22 April), 112.
   The Moore-David Wallace letters on the naming of the
   Edsel have been published in The New Yorker (13 April 1957).

2 ANON. "Axis of the Hairfine Moon." The Times Literary Supplement, no. 2908 (22 November), p. 704.
      Moore's work embodies wit, style, and imagination. But
   central to it is her counting of syllables, "her concession
   to Poetry." It is "part of the furniture of that astringent
   world which art entered during the second decade of the
   twentieth century." Although Moore's poems often seen "cam-
   eos," they are "universal enough." But, as a reading of
   "Tom Fool at Jamaica" in Like a Bulwark reveals, her poems
   at times depend on the notes and fail to cohere. "Values
   in Use," "The Sycamore," and "Blessed Is the Man" are more
   successful and "are evidence of a liveliness and freshness
   of mind scarcely paralleled in a poet of her years."

3 ANON. "The Listener's Book Chronicle." The Listener, 58 (12
   September), 399, 401.
      While some of the poems of Like a Bulwark display Moore's
   strength (that is, "purity and originality of visual imagery, a gift for idiosyncratic aphorism, and a delayed irony
   which is wonderfully counterpointed with the sophisticated
   rhythm of her verse"), others present prosy, raw ideas that
   sound like "William Carlos Williams at his worst."

4 ANON. "Marianne Moore's Poems." In American Writing Today:
   Its Independence and Vigor. Edited by Allan Angoff. Washington Square, New York: New York University Press, pp.
   387-91.
      Reprint of 1936.1.

5 BALABAN, DAN. "A Great American Poetess Remembers the Vil-
   lage." The Village Voice, 6 February, pp. 3, 11.
      Moore misses Greenwich Village but thinks that she could
   not afford it now. In 1918 she and her mother rented an
   apartment on St. Luke's Place, and she worked at the Hudson
   Park Library. Among her acquaintances and friends then were
   Dreiser, Genevieve Taggard, Elinor Wylie, Lola Ridge,
   Maxwell Bodenheim, Stevens, Crane, Williams, Alfred
   Kreymborg, and William Rose Benét. She corresponded with
   Pound but did not meet him until 1936. In 1929 Moore moved
   to Brooklyn.

1957

6   BLACKMUR, R. P. "The Method of Marianne Moore." In his <u>Form and Value in Modern Poetry</u>. Garden City, N.Y.: Doubleday & Co., Anchor Books, pp. 225-52.
    Reprint of 1935.3.

7   BOGAN, LOUISE. "Books: Verse." <u>The New Yorker</u>, 33 (2 March), 111.
    <u>Like a Bulwark</u> presents eleven poems on Moore's "favorite theme of courage linked to excellence."

8   BRINNIN, JOHN MALCOLM. "Marianne Moore's." <u>The Trinity Review</u>, 11 (Spring-Summer), 27.
    Poem.

9   CONQUEST, ROBERT. "Intercontinental Missiles." <u>The Spectator</u>, 199 (11 October), 488.
    An exception to the general accessibility of American culture to England is American poetry. Large parts of it are "extraordinarily alien." I admire but am baffled by Moore's "curious constructions." Unlike English poetry, they lack "a public voice." <u>Like a Bulwark</u> is a minor addition to <u>Collected Poems</u>.

10 DEUTSCHE, BABETTE. "Medley of Marianne Moore." <u>New York Herald Tribune Book Review</u>, 33 (27 January), 5.
    Moore's reticence can be seen in the use of quotation and notes, the unobtrusive rhyme and meter, and the slimness of <u>Like a Bulwark</u>. We could do with less reticence. Moore's primary concern is moral.

11 FALLON, PADRAIC. "Verse Chronicle." <u>The Dublin Magazine</u>, NS 32 (October-December), 36-37.
    <u>Like a Bulwark</u> continues the tone of Moore's earlier poetry. Moore is "an exquisite verbalist," at her best when concentrating on the visual.

12 FOWLIE, WALLACE. "Jorge Guillén, Marianne Moore, T. S. Eliot: Some Recollections." <u>Poetry</u>, 90 (May), 105-107.
    In my meetings with Moore, she struck me as "one constantly collecting and arranging precious bits for the composing of a future poem." In life and art, she exercises a careful attention to detail.

13 FRASER, G. S. "Modern Poetry: The American Accent." <u>Partisan Review</u>, 24 (Winter), 136-37.
    Moore's poetry in <u>Like a Bulwark</u> seems at once something homemade and the product of a virtuoso. Her scrupulous precision in treating things renews them for our perception.

14 FULLER, ROY. Review of Like a Bulwark. The London Magazine, 4 (November), 87, 89.
Like a Bulwark does not show Moore at her best. Its poems are uncompromisingly "complicated and elliptical," depending heavily on the notes, and are less successful in assimilating their material and in offering "striking observations." But she can still make poetry out of the ordinary.

15 GAJDUSEK, ROBERT. Review of Like a Bulwark. The American Scholar, 26 (Spring), 258, 260.
The poems of Like a Bulwark have an "intensity of vision" that demonstrates one of the richest and most precise sensibilities writing today.

16 HOLMES, JOHN. "If Not Silence, Then Restraint." The Trinity Review, 11 (Spring-Summer), 28.
Poem.

17 HOUGH, GRAHAM. Review of Like a Bulwark. Encounter, 9 (November), 83-84.
Moore, like Robert Graves, "has been working in an almost unchanged manner, unaffected by fashion and movements, for over forty years." Moore has a "dry intelligence and ...odd individuality of perception," which are "useful adjuncts to poetic procedure" but not, as she uses them, substitutes for it. Her syllabic meter is arbitrary and merely visual. She does not weave together with skill her quotations and "finicky erudition." But her good reputation belongs to an earlier period, which valued novelty produced by intelligence and devoid of emotion and traditional sonority.

18 KOCH, KENNETH. "New Books by Marianne Moore and W. H. Auden." Poetry, 90 (April), 47-50.
The poems of Like a Bulwark are not among Moore's best. Perhaps translating La Fontaine has caused her to make the moral content of her art obtrusive--even conventional and sentimental.

19 McDONALD, GERALD D. Brief notice of Like a Bulwark. Library Journal, 82 (1 March), 679.
Like a Bulwark is "an important book containing some of the very best of Marianne Moore."

20 MORSE, SAMUEL FRENCH. Review of Predilections. The Trinity Review, 11 (Spring-Summer), 28.

1957

> Moore's criticism, unlike impressionistic and self-con-
> scious criticism, draws attention to, not away from, the
> works being discussed.

21   MUIR, EDWIN. "Kinds of Poetry." New Statesman, 54 (28 Sep-
>   tember), 391-92.
>   Moore's poetry is "calm," a place of interest rather
>   than emotion. Moore is like Gibbon but with the seventeenth-
>   century fondness for "surprising allusion." She sees things
>   clearly and discovers their moral qualities. The poems in
>   Like a Bulwark are "beautifully wrought."

22   NICHOLS, LEWIS. "Miss Moore." The New York Times Book Review,
>   10 November, p. 8.
>   Now that the Dodgers have left Brooklyn, the only insti-
>   tution remaining is Moore, who will be seventy Tuesday.
>   Moore says that she has no plans for another major work
>   like her translation of La Fontaine.

23   OLSON, ELDER. "The Poetry of Marianne Moore." Chicago Review,
>   11 (Spring), 100-104.
>   While most modern writers are still in the romantic tra-
>   dition, Moore is writing in the classical. Her poems do
>   not deal with the extraordinary or contain images distorted
>   by imagination or emotion. The result is a remarkable va-
>   riety in the poems of Like a Bulwark. In each poem, Moore
>   is herself, employing "an imagination with more precision
>   than sensation because it is governed by an intellect more
>   precise than either." As in "Tom Fool at Jamaica," Moore
>   makes us see what she sees. She is difficult, not obscure.
>   Reprinted: 1976.5.

24   RAGO, HENRY. "That the Delight Be in the Instruction and the
>   Instruction in the Delight." The Trinity Review, 11 (Spring-
>   Summer), 24.
>   Moore's poetry teaches us "strength, honesty, taste."

25   REES, RALPH. "The Armor of Marianne Moore." The Bucknell Re-
>   view, 7 (May), 27-40.
>   Armor, a frequent motif in Moore's poetry, appears in
>   the descriptions of animals and in her own "reticence and
>   need for expression." One technique she uses to armor her
>   verse is "indirection" of imagery, syntax, and poetic form
>   --a technique seen in "Peter," "The Pangolin," "The Mind
>   Is an Enchanting Thing," and "Spenser's Ireland." Another
>   technique is "compression" of statement--seen in "To a
>   Snail" and in the revision of "Nevertheless" and "Nine

Nectarines." Along with armor go an admiration for struggle, an attendant faith, and an implied "movement toward self-sufficiency."

26 ROSENTHAL, M. L. "Ladies Day on Parnassus." The Nation, 184 (16 March), 240.
Like a Bulwark praises "the durable in life, the richly common."

27 SARGEANT, WINTHROP. "Profiles: Humility, Concentration, and Gusto." The New Yorker, 32 (16 February), 38-40, 42, 44, 47-49, 52, 54, 56, 58-60, 63-64, 67-68, 70, 75, 76-77.
Moore is a "phenomenon of some complexity." She is regarded by some as the greatest American poet, by others as a cute old lady, by others as a chatterbox, and by others as a genteel neighbor or devout parishioner. Her poems suggest that she is remote, and her Brooklyn apartment confirms it. It is restrictively snug, crowded with books and things. Her talk is diverse and associative. Family relationships have been especially important to her. Reviewing her life and work, one can see her as "a charmingly quixotic intellectual flirt, seeming...to tease those who put their faith in humdrum logic but at the same time to regard them with admiration and a certain coquettish timidity."

28 SCOTT, WINFIELD TOWNLEY. "A Place for the Genuine." The Saturday Review, 40 (2 February), 17-18.
The question of the value of Moore's poetry is still unsolved, despite her awards and celebrity. The work has not been examined. Instead, it has been dismissed (as I dismissed it earlier) or has been obscured by praise so that one person's finical poet becomes another's fastidious poet. In the long run, her poems are likely to be valued for their didacticism ("In Distrust of Merits") rather than their eccentric observation ("A Carriage from Sweden"). The poems in Like a Bulwark, like her others, have the qualities of feeling, precision, humility, concentration, and gusto. The first quality is "the one to bet on."
Excerpted: 1960.17.

29 STEVENS, WALLACE. "A Poet That Matters." In his Opus Posthumous. Edited by Samuel French Morse. New York: Alfred A Knopf, pp. 247-54.
Reprint of 1935.20.

30 TOMLINSON, CHARLES. "Abundance, Not Too Much: The Poetry of Marianne Moore." The Sewanee Review, 65 (October-December), 677-87.

1957

The best poems in <u>Like a Bulwark</u> are successful exercises in Moore's "system of transition between fact and moral fantasy." The system was evident in <u>Selected Poems</u>, which, with poems like "Black Earth," "Silence," and "The Steeple-Jack," established her theme of the relationship between order and spontaneity. <u>What Are Years</u> and <u>Nevertheless</u> show evidence of Moore's attempt to improve on her theme by a willed spontaneity, with the result being the sentimentality and simplification seen in "Keeping Their World Large" and "In Distrust of Merits." Now, in <u>Like a Bulwark</u>, especially in its "Tom Fool at Jamaica," "The Sycamore," and "Apparition of Splendor," Moore re-establishes the limits in which her best work has been done.

31 UPDIKE, JOHN. "Notes." <u>The New Yorker</u>, 32 (26 January), 28-29.
    Moore's notes to <u>Like a Bulwark</u> and John Berryman's to <u>Homage to Mistress Bradstreet</u> are disquieting, a decadent trend following Eliot's masterful use of notes in <u>The Waste Land</u>. But if Moore's poems are a sort of tidy attic, she probably needs the notes as a storeroom.

32 WELLS, HENRY W. "Fastidiousness at a Price." <u>Voices</u>, no. 157 (January-April), pp. 40-42.
    <u>Like a Bulwark</u>, like Moore's other books, shows her strength (a stringent, epigrammatic style) and her weaknesses (lack of emotion and the use of "riddling references").

33 WILLIAMS, WILLIAM CARLOS. "Marianne Moore." <u>The Trinity Review</u>, 11 (Spring-Summer), 24.
    Moore's wit is obvious in "Those Various Scalpels"; her private imagination lies behind "A Talisman." Moore takes me to task for my use of vulgar phrases. I love her.

1958

1 ANON. "Ellis Island: Park, Youth Center, Shrine or--?" <u>The New York Times</u>, 25 May, sec. 6, p. 24.
   Moore was one of six prominent citizens who offered proposals about what should be done with Ellis Island.

2 ANON. "Gathering of Eight Major U.S. Poets 'Pretty Conventional' to Big Audience." <u>The New York Times</u>, 16 November, p. 137.
   Moore was one of eight poets who participated in the poetry festival at Johns Hopkins University.

3   ANON. "Library Lists Verse of Marianne Moore." <u>The New York Times</u>, 3 August, p. 82.
    The New York Public Library has published a bibliography of Moore (1958.16).

4   ANON. "M'Cracken Attacks Ad Agencies' Roles." <u>The New York Times</u>, 7 June, p. 39.
    Moore was awarded an honorary Doctor of Humane Letters degree by Pratt Institute yesterday.

5   ANON. "Marianne Moore Cited." <u>The New York Times</u>, 18 May, p. 52.
    Moore was today announced the winner of the poetry award of the annual Boston Arts Festival. She is the first woman to receive the award.

6   <u>BELOOF, ROBERT</u>. "Prosody and Tone: The 'Mathematics' of Marianne Moore." <u>The Kenyon Review</u>, 20 (Winter), 116–23.
    Moore uses her "syllabic prosody...to minimize the usual rhythmic possibilities of syllabic structure" and thus to approximate free verse, her mathematic tone arising from other techniques. In some later, more lyrical, poems she adheres to her syllabics but does not minimize "the usual syllabic effect."
    Reprinted: 1969.28. Excerpted: 1975.2.

7   BORROFF, MARIE. "Dramatic Structure in the Poetry of Marianne Moore." <u>The Literary Review</u>, 2 (Autumn), 112–23.
    Attracted by striking lines in Moore's poetry, critics have largely ignored her "power of synthesis"--her ability to combine elements into a "dramatic sequence." The cutting of material from "The Steeple-Jack" is evidence of the priority of structure over local felicity of expression. Moore arranges her observations to imply a speaker's mental action. Thus she can use the descriptions of swans in "No Swan So Fine" and "Critics and Connoisseurs" as perceptions with differing motivations. The occasions of Moore's lyrics are the speakers' "interest in moral abstraction." In "Light Is Speech," for example, the speaker's concern is "French culture and the moral values it has historically embodied." Reading Moore's poetry is an act of experiencing "a process of thought" revealed through dramatic structure.

8   ____. "Moore's 'The Icosasphere.'" <u>The Explicator</u>, 16 (January), item 21.
    The difficulty of seeing logical connections and progressions from statement to statement in Moore's "The

1958

Icosasphere" results from her "poetic method." Indeed, the
poem is about integration and failures of it.

9   HEINEY, DONALD. "Marianne Moore." In his <u>Recent American</u>
     <u>Literature</u>. Great Neck, N.Y.: Barron's Educational Series,
     Inc., pp. 537-40, 597.
         Specialized rather than obscure, Moore's poetry is not
     popular. It does not deal with social concerns or with
     "profound philosophical or religious problems"; it describes
     in concrete images "an impressionistic world of the imagin-
     ation." "To a Steam Roller," "Poetry," and "In Distrust of
     Merits" are typical of her work. Includes biographical
     sketch.

10   KENNER, HUGH. "Supreme in Her Abnormality." In his <u>Gnomon</u>:
     <u>Essays on Contemporary Literature</u>. New York: McDowell,
     Obolensky, pp. 189-97.
         Reprint of 1954.16. Excerpted: 1975.2.

11   LEWIS, ANTHONY. "U.S. Asked to End Pound Indictment." <u>The</u>
     <u>New York Times</u>, 15 April, p. 19.
         Moore and other literary figures released today a state-
     ment supporting the move by Pound's lawyer to have the in-
     dictment for treason dismissed. They asked that Pound be
     released from St. Elizabeth's and allowed to return with
     his wife to Italy.

12   NICHOLS, LEWIS. "Day in Boston." <u>The New York Times Book Re-</u>
     <u>view</u>, 29 June, p. 8.
         Moore recently visited Boston, where she received the
     Arts Festival Award and gave a reading in the Public Garden.
     She did not mention the Dodgers or Ted Williams.

13   NORMAN, CHARLES. <u>The Magic-Maker: E. E. Cummings</u>. New York:
     The Macmillan Co., pp. 141, 142, 164, 166-69, 186, 191, 271,
     272, 288, 316, 317, 329, 352.
         Moore was among those who in 1922 gathered often at the
     apartment of Paul Rosenfeld. When Cummings won the Dial
     Award for 1925, Moore accompanied him to his studio to help
     him select a painting to appear in <u>The Dial</u>. He once said
     that Moore's "A Grave" was his favorite poem. Moore owned
     a picture of a rose by Cummings.

14   OLSON, ELDER. "A Valentine for Marianne Moore." <u>Poetry</u>, 91
     (March), 348-49.
         Poem.

15 PHILLIPS, JAMES E. "Introduction." In Idiosyncrasy & Tech-
nique: Inaugurating the Ewing Lectures of the University
of California, Los Angeles, October 3 and 5, 1965 by Marianne
Moore. Berkeley and Los Angeles: University of California
Press, pp. v-vi.
It is an honor to have Moore as the first Ewing lecturer.

16 SHEEHY, EUGENE P. and KENNETH A. LOHF. "The Achievement of
Marianne Moore." Bulletin of the New York Public Library,
62 (March, April, May), 132-49, 183-90, 249-59.
A bibliography of works by and about Moore.
Reprinted: 1958.17.

17 _____. The Achievement of Marianne Moore: A Bibliography,
1907-1957. New York: The New York Public Library, 43 pp.
Reprint with corrections and additions of 1958.16.

18 STAPLETON, LAURENCE. "Marianne Moore and the Element of Prose."
The South Atlantic Quarterly, 57 (Summer), 366-74.
Unlike Pound and Eliot, Moore devoted most of her reviews
and criticism to her contemporaries. And because she lacked
their kind of historical or polemical sense and the "power
of abstract formulation," she surprises us with juxtaposition, insights--as when she links Eliot and Stevens in a
search for "that which will endure." When Moore's criticism
praises, it adds to understanding, including our understanding of her poetic. Her prose rhythms seem of the
seventeenth century; her "propriety and exactitude" remind
us of Jane Austen. For her metaphors she draws on sports,
skills, and art. She combines informal phrasing (often
quoted) with formal logic. Her technical comments on syntax,
rhyme, and rhythm should be of interest to other poets. She
does not separate concern for technique and concern for
substance.

1959

1 ANON. Brief notice of O to Be a Dragon. The Booklist and
Subscription Books Bulletin, 56 (1 November), 148.
Several of the poems "reaffirm the poet's inventiveness
and quick wit."

2 ANON. "Major Poet, Minor Verse." Time, 74 (21 September),
110.
Reaching Moore's Brooklyn apartment [directions are
given] is easier than "reaching the heart of her poetry."

1959

O to Be a Dragon is a poorer road to it than is Collected
Poems.

3   BOGAN, LOUISE. Review of O to Be a Dragon. The New Yorker,
    35 (28 November), 240.
        The book is refreshing.

4   CAREY, SISTER MARY CECILIA. "The Poetry of Marianne Moore:
    A Study of Her Verse, Its Sources, and Its Influences."
    Ph.D. dissertation, University of Wisconsin, 321 pp. Ab-
    stracted in Dissertation Abstracts, 20 (1959), 1023.
        Moore's poems have an organic unity that makes them more
    than mere technical accomplishments. Although one can trace
    influences on her poetry, it remains unique. It combines
    free verse and intellectual rigor. Her themes, often pre-
    sented through animals, are predominantly moral and optimis-
    tic. To contemporary poets, she offers an example of
    artistic integrity.

5   FISCALINI, JANET. "What Exactness Is." The Commonweal, 71
    (20 November), 243-44.
        Style is a matter of moral choice for Moore, though her
    esthetic and moral choices crowd one another in her "home-
    and-library-and-garden world." Her poems, including those
    in the minor O to Be a Dragon, reflect this crowding.

6   HECHT, ANTHONY. "The Anguish of the Spirit and the Letter."
    The Hudson Review, 12 (Winter 1959-60), 594.
        The Society for the Prevention of Cruelty to Animals
    would do well to appropriate Moore's "Saint Nicholas." The
    Society might like all of the poems in O to Be a Dragon.
    Her poem in praise of the Dodgers is a joke in bad taste,
    an act of self-deprecation slipping toward vanity.

7   McBRIDE, HENRY. "The Dial: An Adventure of the 1920s." Art
    News, 58 (Summer), 29.
        The Dial helped Moore win international recognition.
    Alyse Gregory once took Moore to task for the failure of
    "Sea Unicorns and Land Unicorns" to indicate that these
    animals were mythical.

8   ROBIE, BURTON. Brief notice of O to Be a Dragon. Library
    Journal, 84 (1 September), 2506.
        "Highly recommended for all collections," O to Be a Drag-
    on contains poems "seemingly artless but strictly and orig-
    inally composed."

9   RUKEYSER, MURIEL. "The Rhythm Is the Person." Saturday Review, 42 (19 September), 17-18.
    Rhythm and conviction are characteristic of Moore's poetry. In O to Be a Dragon, the poem "In the Public Garden" displays them and has its source in psalms and hymns. Indeed, some of the forms Moore uses, though sometimes thought eccentric, are very close to hymn meters.

10 SAAL, ROLLENE W. Biographical sketch. Saturday Review, 42 (19 September), 17.
    Moore is one of the "elders of modern poetry." Her apartment is filled with souvenirs. She seldom writes more than four poems a year. Acquiring a television set has increased her interest in baseball.

11 SHAPIRO, KARL. "Born of a Lifetime in New York." The New York Times Book Review, 4 October, p. 41.
    Moore is still writing poetry of the 1920s. She is Eliot's "only American disciple," continuing to write "textbook poetry." O to Be a Dragon does contain a perfect poem of her type--"Leonardo da Vinci's." The baseball poem is neither academic nor humorous.

12 UNTERMEYER, LOUIS. "Marianne Moore." In his Lives of the Poets: The Story of One Thousand Years of English and American Poetry. New York: Simon and Schuster, pp. 700-702.
    Moore is modest, calling her work poetry only because there is no other term for it. It is "highly special poetry for specialized tastes."

13 WALSH, CHAD. "Marianne Moore's Fancy." New York Herald Tribune Book Review, 36 (4 October), 7.
    O to Be a Dragon, despite its slimness, seems "an important publishing event." Regardless of her subject, Moore unites "experience, meditation, thought, feeling, rhythm, and diction." "To a Chameleon" is an example of the "lapidary finality" she achieves.

1960

1   ANON. "Poets Get Salute from Eisenhower." The New York Times, 22 January, p. 19.
    Moore, Frost, and Robert Graves were honored guests at the fiftieth aniversary dinner of the Poetry Society of America. Moore received the Society's gold medal.

1960

2   ANON. Review of O to Be a Dragon. The Virginia Quarterly Re-
      view, 36 (Winter), xxii.
          O to Be a Dragon lacks the "vividness and fine humor" of
      Moore's best work.

3   ANON. "75 Alumnae Receive Bryn Mawr Awards." The New York
      Times, 5 June, p. 126.
          Moore was among seventy-five Bryn Mawr alumnae awarded
      citations for distinguished service.

4   BEACH, JOSEPH WARREN. "The Hero." In his Obsessive Images:
      Symbolism in the Poetry of the 1930s and 1940s. Edited by
      William Van O'Connor. Minneapolis: University of Minnesota
      Press, pp. 213-15.
          In her poem "The Hero," Moore presents the hero as a
      person who "sees the ideal essence of experience."

5   BEVINGTON, HELEN. Review of Four Poets on Poetry, edited by
      Don Cameron Allen. The South Atlantic Quarterly, 59 (Sum-
      mer), 452.
          This collection of essays lacks unity. The piece by
      Moore is a brief comment, largely quotation, on Dame Edith
      Sitwell, whose rhythms Moore likes.

6   COLOMBO, JOHN ROBERT. Review of O to Be a Dragon. The Cana-
      dian Forum, 40 (April), 23.
          Like Edith Sitwell, Moore is a "literary lapidarian,"
      a poet interested in "the poetic word qua word."

7   DONOGHUE, DENIS. "For Civility." Poetry, 96 (September), 384
          Moore's essay on Edith Sitwell in Four Poets on Poetry
      is characteristic of Moore in its admirable civility.

8   DUNCAN, ROBERT. "The Maiden." In his The Opening of the
      Field. New York: Grove Press, pp. 27-29.
          Poem.

9   GIBBS, ALONZO. "The Sports Department." Voices, no. 173
      (September-December), pp. 40-41.
          O to Be a Dragon was probably rushed into publication
      "to satisfy a demand for copies of 'Hometown Piece for
      Messrs. Alston and Reese.'" Moore's agile use of meter
      seems like a saving catch in baseball. The poems in this
      volume seem "more brittle than those in Collected Poems."

10 HOFFMAN, DANIEL G. Review of O to Be a Dragon. The Sewanee
      Review, 68 (January-March), 128-30.

Moore creates rather than imposes meaning on the animals in her poetry. Her attention to craft and her "unexampled verbal delicacy and wit, braced by rigorous individualism" are present in O to Be a Dragon.

11 JONES, LLEWELLYN. "Surfaces and Morals." The Humanist, 20 (November-December), 367-68.
    Readers of Moore's poetry too often peer at her "bric-a-brac and small animals" and thereby miss the large issues. In O to Be a Dragon, the poems "Combat Cultural," "Melchoir Vulpius," and "Enough" are important treatments of themes of interest to Humanists.

12 KERMODE, FRANK. "Poetry Chronicle." Partisan Review, 27 (Winter), 160.
    O to Be a Dragon is "radiant, professional, personal, and full of intellect."

13 KUNITZ, STANLEY. "Process and Thing: A Year of Poetry." Harper's Magazine, 221 (September), 96, 98.
    O to Be a Dragon does not "modify Moore's status as a poet," since she is unique. She has an ethical concern for the language.

14 MORSE, SAMUEL FRENCH. "Trusting the Art." Poetry, 96 (May), 112-14.
    O to Be a Dragon contains some of Moore's earliest poems. The new poems seem more detached, more strenuously serious, yet also more playful. Moore does not imitate herself.

15 NORMAN, CHARLES. Ezra Pound. New York: The Macmillan Co., pp. 5, 182, 210-11, 225, 245, 252, 256, 290, 299, 363-64, 439-41, 462.
    Pound met Moore for the first time in 1933 and not again until she visited him in St. Elizabeth's. She sought his help with her translations of La Fontaine.

16 NOWLAN, ALDEN A. "Ten Books of Poetry." The Tamarack Review, no. 16 (Summer), p. 71.
    Although the poems of O to Be a Dragon are "technically the best" of the ten books of poetry under review, they are disappointing. Moore has great craftsmanship--enough to rank her "with the greatest poets in English"--but she lacks vitality. As in "Hometown Piece for Messrs. Alston and Reese," Moore sometimes reduces the "wild and masculine" to the decorative and cute.

1960

17   NYREN, DOROTHY, ed. "Marianne Moore." In A Library of Liter-
      ary Criticism: Modern American Literature. New York:
      Frederick Ungar Publishing Co., pp. 348-51.
          Excerpts from 1922.3, 1925.22, 1928.1, 1937.4, 1940.1,
      1949.2, 1953.13, 1956.17, 1957.28.

18   ROSENTHAL, M. L. "Moore, Cummings, Sandburg, Jeffers." In
      his The Modern Poets: A Critical Introduction. New York:
      Oxford University Press, pp. 140-46.
          Moore, like Pound and Eliot, is a "skilled mechanic" in
      art. Her poem "Camellia Sabina," with its "massing of
      special information, discriminatingly but somewhat arbi-
      trarily selected, and its orchestration, as it were, by a
      witty mind with a fastidious sense of form," is character-
      istic of her work. In poems expressing her views of matters
      philosophical, moral, or esthetic, she makes use of seem-
      ingly overheard and fascinating statements about such
      subjects as ostriches. In poems like "The Wood-Weasel" and
      "His Shield," one finds her admiration for adaptable but
      defended individualism. "To a Steam Roller" has, like much
      of her poetry, "the theme of the negative"--a fastidious
      process of elimination that closes in "on right attitudes
      of taste." Her "unique effects," which give her a super-
      ficial resemblance to Cummings, should not obscure the
      similarities with Stevens, Pound, Eliot, Williams, and even
      Blake.
          Excerpted: 1973.4.

19   SCHWARTZ, DELMORE. "The Art of Marianne Moore." The New Re-
      public, 142 (4 January), 19.
          The poems in O to Be a Dragon "do not represent a further
      development of [Moore's] poetic gifts." (In fact, among
      them is a "bad poem on the Brooklyn Dodgers.") Moore con-
      tinues to write with a "felicitous precision" that is a
      defense of the English language.

20   THORP, WILLARD. "Make It New: Poetry, 1920-1950." In his
      American Writing in the Twentieth Century. Cambridge:
      Harvard University Press, pp. 211-14.
          Typically, Moore begins with an object, adds "miscella-
      neous bits of information," and concludes with a moral.
      Her poetry has "a music which only a great metrist could
      compose."

21   WARLOW, FRANCIS W. "Marianne Moore: Unfalsifying Sun and
      Solid Gilded Star." Ph.D. dissertation, University of
      Pennsylvania, 442 pp. Abstracted in Dissertation Abstracts,
      20 (1960), 2814.

Biographical information supports the conclusion that
Moore is a Christian, a moralist, a rationalist-scientist,
and an artist. During her career, she has remained conservative in values. Her early poetry was first epigrammatic
and formally idiosyncratic and then more expansive, in form
and subject. Later, it returned to the eccentric formal
patterns. In addition to showing French influences, she
combines the American metaphysical tradition and English
Estheticism. She has chosen unconventional forms to present
her conventional values.

1961

1 ALDEN, ROBERT. "Advertising: War Drums on the Potomac?" The
   New York Times, 26 February, sec. 3, p. 12.
       Moore joined other public figures in voicing opinions
   about advertising. She objected to cigarette advertising.

2 ANON. Brief Notice of A Marianne Moore Reader. The Booklist
   and Subscription Books Bulletin, 58 (15 September), 56
       The Reader provides a "generous sampling" of Moore's
   work.

3 ANON. Review of A Marianne Moore Reader. The New Yorker, 37
   (16 December), 207.
       It is "a gallant and life-enhancing volume."

4 BENET, ROSEMARY. Review of A Marianne Moore Reader. Book of
   the Month Club News, November, p. 6.
       The collection is delightful and reflects "one of the
   most original, lively minds of our time."

5 CANNELL, KATHLEEN. "Caught in 'a Maze, a Trap, a Web.'" The
   Christian Science Monitor, Eastern edition, 30 November,
   p. 18.
       A Marianne Moore Reader is "a guide to the neophyte and
   a manual for the professional." Moore is, without being
   self righteous, devoted to morality. Humor humanizes her
   scrupulosity.

6 DEMPSEY, DAVID. "In a Collector's Pleasure Is Pleasure to
   Share." The New York Times Book Review, 3 December, pp.
   3, 30.
       The Marianne Moore Reader shows that poetry and prose
   "can be both contemporary and poetic."

1961

7   DUNCAN, ROBERT. "Ideas of the Meaning of Form." Kulchur, no.
      4, pp. 65-69.
          Moore is a conventional poet by nature, not "by social
      class or prejudice." Increasingly, her poetry has come to
      identify truth with that which resists experience rather
      than with experience. And it has come to sacrifice "char-
      acter...to public personality."

8   HALL, DONALD. "The Art of Poetry IV: Marianne Moore." Paris
      Review, no. 26 (Summer-Fall), pp. 41-66.
          The most extensive interview with Moore. Concerns her
      life and art.
          Reprinted: 1961.9, 1963.8, 1969.28.

9   _____. "Interview with Donald Hall." In A Marianne Moore
      Reader. New York: The Viking Press, pp. 251-73.
          Reprint of 1961.8.

10 HYMAN, STANLEY EDGAR. "Marianne Moore at Seventy-Four." The
      New Leader, 44 (27 November), 25-26.
          A Marianne Moore Reader is a fine "retrospective show."
          Reprinted: 1966.14.

11 NORMAN, GERTRUDE. "To a Young Roach." Chelsea, no. 10 (Sep-
      tember) p. 74.
          Poem about and in imitation of Moore.

12 PEARCE, ROY HARVEY. "Marianne Moore." In his The Continuity
      of American Poetry. Princeton: Princeton University Press,
      pp. 366-75.
          Moore's poetry is modest, not given to cosmic insights.
      In Selected Poems, one can see the world of her poems as
      "a series of assemblages not of ideas but of things in them-
      selves" (as Williams saw them) or as scene and occasion for
      meditations (as Eliot saw them). Her later poetry is more
      obviously meditative: she makes a scene "yield a meaning."
      In "No Swan So Fine," Moore, unlike Williams, can insist
      "on having ideas about the thing," and unlike Eliot, can
      have meditation defined rather than released by the thing.
      In rhetorical poems like "What Are Years," she meditates
      free of things. In later and better poems like "Neverthe-
      less," she uses observation of things as "a means to, not
      a mode of, insight."
          Reprinted: 1969.28.

13 POORE, CHARLES. "Books of the Times." The New York Times, 21
      December, p. 25.
          In A Marianne Moore Reader, defending herself against
      those who criticized her for extolling President Eisenhower,

1962

Moore coins the phrase "political esthetes." The phrase typifies her independence and effectiveness as a poet. The Reader contains Moore's "wonderful translations of the Fables," her "high-hearted" correspondence with the Ford Motor Company, poetic tributes to baseball players (which exceed those given to Yeats, Eliot, Shakespeare, and the like), and the Paris Review interview. Moore praises Brooklyn "with the drop-of-a-tricorn hat enthusiasm." We admire her "infinite capacity for ardor."

14 ROBIE, BURTON A. Brief notice of A Marianne Moore Reader. Library Journal, 86 (1 November), 3790.
"For all literature collections," the book provides a feast.

15 SCOTT, WINFIELD TOWNLEY. "A Sampler of Delights." New York Herald Tribune Books, 38 (26 November), 9.
The sample of Moore's work in A Marianne Moore Reader reveals Moore's "magpie of a mind." She is a precise magpie.

1962

1 ANON. "Outdoor Readings of Poetry Started." The New York Times, 18 June, p. 20.
Moore was the first to read in the city's first series of outdoor poetry readings last night at the New School for Social Research.

2 ANON. "Pupils at Poetry Reading." The New York Times, 7 April, p. 24.
Members of Eastern District High School's Problems in American Democracy class have objected to characterization of pupils in the New York Times article on Moore's visit to the school (1962.23).

3 ANON. Review of A Marianne Moore Reader. The Virginia Quarterly Review, 38 (Summer), lxxxi.
There are not enough poems in the Reader, but the best are there. The Ford correspondence could have been omitted.

4 ANON. "70 Attend Birthday Party for Marianne Moore, 75." The New York Times, 16 November, p. 28.
Seventy fellow artists, including Auden and Robert Lowell, joined Moore in celebrating her seventy-fifth birthday last night at a dinner sponsored by the American Academy of Arts and Letters and the National Institute of Arts and Letters.

1962

5   AUDEN, W. H. "Marianne Moore." In The Dyer's Hand and Other
    Essays. New York: Random House, pp. 296-305.
        I used to find Moore's poetry difficult, but her tone of
    voice attracted me. Today I find her a "pleasure to read."
    Moore is "a naturalist," writing about the animals she likes.
    She also writes about human beings, and her poetry often
    has as its theme "the Good Life."

6   BARRETT, WILLIAM. Review of A Marianne Moore Reader. Atlantic
    Monthly, 209 (February), 121
        The combination of Moore's poetry and prose creates a
    unified work of "an extraordinary poetic sensibility.'

7   BRUMBAUGH, THOMAS. "In Pursuit of Miss Moore." The Mississippi
    Quarterly, 15 (Spring), 74-80.
        An Account of a long correspondence with Moore on matters
    biographical and literary. Moore's letters are printed.

8   DICKEY, JAMES. Review of A Marianne Moore Reader. The Sewanee
    Review, 70 (July-September), 499-503.
        Moore's poems, composed of odd facts and dazzling de-
    scription, make the world "interesting." There are two
    dangers to her method: that of "disappearing behind her
    quotation" and that of uninspired yoking together of dis-
    parate objects, even when the syllabic verse makes them
    seem to belong together. Moore's essays are like her po-
    ems--packed with quotations. Her essay on Pound is "Pound
    writing on himself as he should have written." Her trans-
    lations of La Fontaine may be more Moore than La Fontaine.
    The inclusion of the Ford letters is regrettable.
        Reprinted: 1968.18. Excerpted: 1973.4.

9   DUDEK, LOUIS. Review of A Marianne Moore Reader. The Canadian
    Forum, 42 (September), 135.
        The influence of Moore is healthy. She "has purified the
    language." She is "an American realist" in that she uses
    symbols in the service of "the rational intellect." Her
    poetry is not obscure, just more "precise and exact" than
    we are. Moore has avoided the triviality that is one of
    the dangers of realism, but she "is just a bit eccentric."

10 FAIRCHILD, HOXIE NEALE. "Lords of a New Language." In his
    Religious Trends in English Poetry. Vol. 5: 1800-1920,
    Gods of a Changing Poetry. New York: Columbia University
    Press, pp. 568-73, 576.
        Moore's verse has changed little since 1921. Although,
    like the imagists, she renders objects precisely, she does
    so in the service of understanding: her eye serves her

1962

brain. Her need to preserve her integrity is seen in the
"technical obstacles" she puts in our way. She does not
make a religion out of art, though her esthetic is "poten-
tially religious."

11   FISCALINI, JANET. "Our Miss Moore." The Commonweal, 75 (26
     January), 473-75.
        There is a whimsicality in Moore that appears in her work
     now that she is a legend. It is found in her occasional
     lapses into over-elaborate imagery and eccentric diction.
     A Marianne Moore Reader is a generous, sometimes too gener-
     ous, selection of her work.

12   HARTSOCK, MILDRED. "Marianne Moore: A 'Salvo of Barks.'"
     Bucknell Review, 11 (December), 14-37.
        With few exceptions, the criticism of Moore is "a strange
     amalgam of patronizing praise and uneasy insistence upon her
     limitations." Critics have shown amazement at her use of
     varied subject matter and her allusions to prose documents,
     and they have insisted that she is idiosyncratic, by which
     they imply a limitation. They neglect to see that Moore is
     a "precisionist" whose allusions and imagery reflect her
     belief that man must view the world as it is. Although
     critics pronounce her lacking in feeling, she is open to
     life, even its chaos. The armored animals that figure in a
     number of her poems are engaged in life--the armor indicating
     intensity more than remoteness. Moore is more like the
     Hebrews and Germans, who combined emotion with exactness of
     detail, than like the Greeks, who distrusted anything com-
     plex. Often called a minor poet, she writes with major
     themes--about the whole "range of human problems and human
     values." Charges by such critics as Yvor Winters (1947.6)
     that her works lack unity are failures of criticism, not
     of the poems, as an analysis of "Marriage" and "An Octopus"
     demonstrates. Finally, although critics have called her
     verse prose, it is the work of "a virtuoso with sound-
     variations." She is a major poet.

13   JACKSON, KATHERINE. "Books in Brief." Harper's Magazine, 224
     (February), 110.
        A Marianne Moore Reader is delightful.

*14 JOOST, NICHOLAS. "The Pertinence of Marianne Moore's Notes to
     'The Jerboa.'" Delta Epsilon Sigma Bulletin, 7 (May), 1-30.
        Cited in Lewis Leary, Articles on American Literature,
     1950-1967 (Durham, N.C.: Duke University Press, 1970).

1962

15   JOSEPHSON, MATTHEW. <u>Life among the Surrealists: A Memoir</u>.
      New York: Holt, Rinehart and Winston, pp. 154-55, 160-63,
      192, 230, 295-97, 390.
          My poem "In a Cafe," a spoof on serious poetry, was re-
      garded by Moore as "an achievement of the highest order."
      (While I admired her sometimes poetic observations, I re-
      garded her as "old fashioned.") Later when she discovered
      the content of the poem, Moore "heaped reproaches upon me
      for hours on end." In 1926 Hart Crane complained to me
      about Moore's revisions of his "Wine Menagerie." After I
      offered to buy the poem back from the <u>Dial,</u> she got assur-
      ances from Crane that he had not asked me to intercede.
      Thereafter, her "editorial intervention gradually
      diminished."

16   KENNEDY, X. J. "Marianne Moore." <u>The Minnesota Review</u>, 2
      (Spring), 369-76.
          Only "a scoundrel or a clod" could fail to admire Moore's
      work. It is not song (though it contains technical tri-
      umphs, especially in rhyme), nor is it the product of a
      "sweetly smiling maiden-lady." Her juxtapositions are
      logical and metaphoric, not eccentric. Her poetry is modest.
      Her intricate stanzas, prosaism, and delight in science
      recall Donne, Herbert, and Vaughan. And her descriptions
      of nature are exact and imaginative.

17   KENNER, HUGH. "Care, Not Madness." <u>National Review</u>, 12 (24
      April), 294, 296.
          Moore's poetry enacts "the art of coping" with the mis-
      cellaneous facts that crowd our lives. She was more suc-
      cessful in her pre-1951 poetry, but even poems collected
      later, some of which are reprinted in <u>A Marianne Moore</u>
      <u>Reader,</u> "illustrate her concern for criteria that matter."
      "Style" and "Propriety," for example, display her method
      of combining fact and art.

18   KNOLL, ROBERT E., ed. In <u>McAlmon and the Lost Generation: A</u>
      <u>Self Portrait</u>. Lincoln: University of Nebraska Press, pp.
      108, 141, 146, 378.
          The character Martha Wallus in McAlmon's novel <u>Post-Ado-</u>
      <u>lescence</u> (Paris: Contact Publishing Co, [1923]) is based
      on Moore.

19   O'CONNOR, WILLIAM VAN. "The Recent Contours of the Muse."
      <u>Saturday Review,</u> 45 (6 January), 71
          Since Moore is now an institution, it is appropriate that
      there is now <u>A Marianne Moore Reader</u>. In her criticism,
      Moore is "an explicator of the self-respecting heart."

20 O'DOHERTY, BRIAN. "Marianne Moore, Turning 75, Remains as
    Discursive as Ever. Telephone Interview with Busy Poet
    Produces Her Views on Baseball, Floyd Patterson and Verse
    Style." The New York Times, 15 November, 39.
        Moore, seventy-five years old today, offered comments on
    baseball, boxing, and writing. Her comments on writing have
    to do with accent, pattern, and compression.

21 PERKINS, ANNE. Review of A Marianne Moore Reader. Jubilee,
    9 (March), 50.
        A "love and respect for words" is evident in this
    collection.

22 RENICKE, SUE. "Moore's 'The Fish.'" The Explicator, 21 (Sep-
    tember), item 7.
        The theme of "The Fish" is "the paradox of destruction
    and endurance." The images of the cliff and the fish are
    united by the observer's "central consciousness that iden-
    tifies itself with the sea."

23 ROBERTSON, NAN. "Gum-Popping Youths Yield to Marianne Moore."
    The New York Times, 22 March, p. 37.
        Yesterday, Moore spoke to one thousand teenagers at
    Eastern District High School in Brooklyn. She commented on
    poems that had won a school contest and on how she judges
    poetry.

24 SHANKAR, D. A. "The Poetry of Marianne Moore." The Literary
    Criterion, 5 (Winter), 141-47.
        Like Henry James, Moore has been damned for decorum.
    Central to her poetry is observation. She does not use
    objects or animals for symbolic import but observes "so
    passionately and objectively" that they "assume a spiritual
    reality." While other American poets either talk down or
    talk to themselves, Moore has achieved Pound's ideal of the
    conversational style.

1963

1 ANON. "Brandeis Presents Annual Art Awards." The New York
    Times, 1 May, p. 32.
        Yesterday, Moore received a Creative Arts award from
    Brandeis University.

2 ANON. "The Children's Christmas Book Bag." The Christian
    Century 80 (18 December), 1586.

1963

>   This season Moore's <u>Puss in Boots, The Sleeping Beauty,</u>
>   <u>& Cinderella</u> is the most interesting of Macmillan's series
>   of fairy tales.

3   BISHOP, CLAIRE HUCHET. "A Selected List of Children's Books."
     <u>The Commonweal</u>, 79 (15 November), 232.
>   Moore's retelling of <u>Puss in Boots, The Sleeping Beauty,</u>
>   <u>& Cinderella</u> is "sensitive and authentic."

4   CECILIA, SISTER MARY. "The Poetry of Marianne Moore." <u>Thought</u>,
     38 (Autumn), 354-74.
>   Moore's poems reflect no "personal spiritual struggle or
>   conflict." Moore searches not for faith but "for that self
>   realization which faith guarantees." The need for moral
>   courage is one major theme. Her poems on war, love, hate,
>   and death are still concerned with "man's dignity as man
>   and with his realization of his God-given potential."
>   Critics generally overlook Moore's concern with "the in-
>   vestigation of reality." For her, ideas inhere in facts,
>   poetic and nonpoetic. Her belief that emotion finds ex-
>   pression in restraint is evident in her review of Stevens
>   and in "Silence." As her choice of "What Are Years" as
>   her best poem indicates, she does not reject emotion but
>   thinks it best combined with reason. Through the years her
>   poems have shown an increase in emotional treatment, leading
>   some critics to charge her with sentimentality just as they
>   once charged her with "emotional frigidity." But she inte-
>   grates emotion and intellect, as in "Apparition of Splendor"
>   and "Bird-Witted," for example. So too does she integrate
>   moral qualities, as in "The Jerboa," "Sea Unicorns and Land
>   Unicorns," "His Shield," and other poems. The increasingly
>   didactic tone of <u>Like a Bulwark</u> may be the result of her
>   increasing seriousness and her translating La Fontaine.
>   Although some of her work suffers from her narrow range of
>   experience and from obscurity caused by too great a regard
>   for precision, her most successful poems are "correlative
>   intellectual-emotional-verbal" presentations.

5   DAVENPORT, G[UY]. "Books in Brief." <u>National Review</u>, 14 (26
     February), 169.
>   <u>The Absentee</u> captures Maria Edgeworth's "tone and set-
>   ting." The Victorian sentimentality and perception are
>   welcome.

6   ENGEL, BERNARD. "Marianne Moore and 'Objectivism.'" <u>Papers</u>
     <u>of the Michigan Academy of Science, Arts, and Letters</u>, 48
     (1962 meeting), 657-64.

A paradox underlies Moore's work: while she wants to
advocate values (including "courage, independence, respon-
sibility, genuineness, and a certain ardor in the conduct
of one's life"), she adheres to the principles of Objectivism and its insistence on presentation of "the thing
itself." The paradox produces a poetry of analogy. Her
early poetry often uses implied analogies between the objects presented and the ethical realm. Later poems are
more direct in commentary, subordinating analogy rather
than being controlled by it. The poem "Melanchthon" is
both an "example of her effort to use analogy without being
dominated by it" and a statement "of faith in the existence
of a power underlying and superior to the appearances of
life in the world."
Incorporated with revisions in 1964.9.

7   GREENE, ELLIN PETERSON. Brief notice of Puss in Boots, The
    Sleeping Beauty, & Cinderella. Library Journal, 88 (15
    September), 3354.
       In retelling Perrault's stories Moore follows the orig-
    inal closely but produces not the most readable version.
    It is recommended for "additional purchase only."

8   HALL, DONALD H. "Marianne Moore." In Writers at Work: The
    Paris Review Interviews. Second series. New York: The
    Viking Press, pp. 62–87.
       Reprint of 1961.8.

9   JARRELL, RANDALL. "Fifty Years of American Poetry." Prairie
    Schooner, 37 (Spring), 15–17.
       Incorporates a reprint of 1952.25. Reprinted: 1964.17,
    1969.14. Excerpted in 1974.2.

10 KENNER, HUGH. "Meditation and Enactment." Poetry, 102 (May),
    109–115.
       Unobtrusive rhyme and syllabic patterning of stanzas are
    part of Moore's "conscious fastidiousness" that enacts vir-
    tue by concealing the art through which she presents her
    observations. A Marianne Moore Reader includes some--not
    enough--of Moore's poems that do this well, and it provides
    a longer printer's measure to display the visual aspect of
    her poems. It also includes some recent poems, those written
    for the New Yorker that seem mannerism imposed on platitude.
    Reprinted: 1969.28.

11 LASK, THOMAS. "Books for Younger Readers." The New York Times
    Book Review, 13 October, p. 30.

1963

          The prose of Moore's translations of <u>Puss in Boots, The Sleeping Beauty, & Cinderella</u> is clear. Hers should become the standard versions.

12   LIBBY, MARGARET SHERWOOD. "Three Small Gems Repolished." <u>The Sunday</u> (New York) <u>Herald Tribune Book World</u>, 29 December, p. 13.
          Moore captures Perrault's sophisticated, courtly style in her <u>Puss in Boots, The Sleeping Beauty, & Cinderella</u>.

13   MAXWELL, EMILY. Review of <u>Puss in Boots, The Sleeping Beauty, & Cinderella</u>. <u>The New Yorker</u>, 39 (30 November), 225.
          This book is for adults as well as children. Moore's style makes the stories new.

14   MILLER, LOIS. "I Went to the Animal Fair: An Analysis of Marianne Moore's 'The Monkeys.'" <u>The English Journal</u>, 52 (January), 66-67.
          The animals in "The Monkeys" are presented in parade. In the second half of the poem, they become the spectators. The cat chides us for our pedantic approach to art, an approach that excludes him.

15   NEMEROV, HOWARD. "A Few Bricks from Babel." In his <u>Poetry and Fiction: Essays</u>. New Brunswick: Rutgers University Press, pp. 357-65.
          Reprint of 1954.21.

16   RICHARDS, I. A. "For Marianne Moore on Her Seventy-Fifth Birthday: Relaxed Terza Rima." <u>Poetry</u>, 101 (March), 410-11.
          Poem.

17   SHEEHAN, ETHNA. "<u>America</u> Balances Books for the Children." <u>America</u>, 109 (16 November), 658.
          Moore's translation of <u>Puss in Boots, The Sleeping Beauty, & Cinderella</u> retains Perrault's spirit and style. Unfortunately it includes "the gruesome ogre-ending of <u>The Sleeping Beauty</u>."

18   SIMPSON, LOUIS. "Poetry Chronicle." <u>The Hudson Review</u>, 16 (Spring), 131-32.
          Modern poetry lacks criticism. The younger poets are judged not by the middle generation (for example, Theodore Roethke) but by the minor poets of the twenties (for example, Moore).

19   UNALI, LINA. "Marianne Moore." Studi Americani, no. 9, pp.
     377-410.
          Williams and Pound have acknowledged the central impor-
     tance of Moore in twentieth-century American poetry. Her
     diary contains facts about her life that are reflected in
     her poetry, which uses memory as its material. Poems like
     "An Octopus" and "To a Snail" are statements of her esthe-
     tic. (As an appendix, Unali includes, under the title
     "Dai Reading Transcripts di Marianne Moore," pp. [411-23],
     excerpts from Moore's reading diaries, or commonplace
     books.)

20   WASSERSTROM, WILLIAM, ed. A Dial Miscellany. Syracuse: Syra-
     cuse University Press, 1963, pp. xv, xvi.
          In editing the Dial, Moore followed Scofield Thayer's
     instructions. Before being announced as acting editor,
     Moore received from the Dial praise grander than any pre-
     viously given her in America.

21   WASSERSTROM, WILLIAM. "Marianne Moore, The Dial, and Kenneth
     Burke." Western Humanities Review, 17 (Summer), 249-62.
          Until 1922, the Dial devoted its attention to Eliot.
     Then it shifted its allegiance to Moore and later to Kenneth
     Burke. Despite these shifts and the assumption of editor-
     ship by Moore in 1925, the Dial remained devoted to the
     "romantic doctrine" that civilization might be saved by the
     "nurture and study of the 'creative and critical arts.'"
     Moore's poetry, like the Dial, sought to draw "on all as-
     pects of national life." If, under her editorship, scruple
     won over daring in the demand for revisions of contributions
     (e.g., in Crane's "Wine Menagerie" and in works by Alfred
     Kreymborg, Archibald MacLeish, Thomas Mann, and others) and
     in the rejection of a section of Joyce's Work in Progress,
     it did not interfere with the printing of critical studies
     by Valéry, I. A. Richards, Conrad Aiken, Yvor Winters,
     Eliot, and Burke--all of whom sought to define the nature
     of poetry, its relation to science, and other essential
     questions of literary theory. (At the same time, it could
     include "other kinds of talk"--Williams' for example.)
     Moore was instrumental in securing the 1929 Dial Award for
     Burke, whom she saw as the only American critic likely to
     "reconcile letters and culture, science and imagination in
     a single theory of literary value."
          Reprinted: 1963.22.

22   _____. "The Mark of a Poet: Marianne Moore." In his The
     Time of the Dial. Syracuse: Syracuse University Press,
     pp. 109-31, passim.
          Reprint of 1963.21.

1963

23   WILLIAMS, WILLIAM CARLOS. "Marianne Moore." In A Dial Mis-
     cellany. Edited by William Wasserstrom. Syracuse: Syra-
     cuse University Press, pp. 232-40.
     Reprint of 1925.20.

1964

1   AIKEN, CONRAD. "What's under That Tricorne Hat?" In Fest-
    schrift (1964.33), pp. 31-32.
        I still remember Moore's Poems. John Gould Fletcher,
    Eliot, Harold Monro, and I discussed it with delight. I
    was the first to discover the syllabic principle of her
    verse. And I recall our meetings when she was editor of
    the Dial.

2   BURKE, KENNETH. "She Taught Me to Blush." In Festschrift
    (1964.33), pp. 61
        Working with Moore on the Dial allowed me "to appreciate,
    day by day, the ingenuity and scrupulosity of her ways."
    She combines the ethical and esthetic.

3   BYNNER, WITTER. "When I Met Marianne Moore." In Festschrift
    (1964.33), p. 89.
        I have a vivid and early memory of Moore, a priestess
    whose "name still strikes in me my old deference toward"
    her.

4   CHAKRAVARTY, AMIYA. "Marianne Moore: Only in Pure Sanskrit."
    In Festschrift (1964.33), pp. 94-99.
        Moore's verse broke into the world of "antique modernism"
    that existed at Oxford in the early thirties. She went be-
    yond imagism by making "a passionate correleation which the
    imagists often suggested but did not explicate."

5   COFFIN, PATRICIA. "Upon Seeing Marianne Moore at a Steuben
    Press Party." Prairie Schooner, 38 (Fall), 241.
        Poem.

6   COLUM, PADRAIC. Comment. In Festschrift (1964.33), pp.
    117-18.
        Moore's poetry is unique, a kind of "description by re-
    creation."

7   COWLEY, MALCOLM. "Speech Delivered at Dinner Meeting of the
    National Institute of Arts and Letters on the Occasion of
    Marianne Moore's 75th Birthday, November 15, 1962." In
    Festschrift (1964.33), pp. 120-21.

1964

As editor of the <u>Dial</u>, Moore "filled one with perfect
assurance of her discriminating taste and complete integrity," even when one disagreed with her on some matter, as
I once did. We regard Moore with "affection and respect."

8   EBERHART, RICHARD. "A Memoir." In <u>Festschrift</u> (1964.33),
    pp. 72-73.
    I have several fond memories of Moore.

9   ENGEL, BERNARD. <u>Marianne Moore</u>. Twayne's United States Au-
    thors Series, no. 54. New York: Twayne Publishers, 176 pp.
    Despite the modern critical view that poems <u>are</u> rather
    than <u>mean</u>, Moore's poetry examines and affirms values.
    While themselves conventional, the values are made new in
    her "poetic realization" of them. Yet, as an Objectivist,
    she asserts cautiously--through paradox, induction, analogy,
    and juxtaposition. Her style is one of discipline and re-
    straint. Central to her work is a belief in "the unity of
    spirit and matter" and in the necessary consequences in
    human behavior of that unity. Her work may be divided into
    three periods. The early period culminates in <u>Selected Po-
    ems</u> and shows her admiration for "an aloof individualism
    that would armor the self against assaults of ambition,
    possessions, and other people." The middle period, repre-
    sented by the new poems in <u>Collected Poems</u>, finds her still
    concerned with armoring but also more "understanding of
    man's moral handicaps and thus of his moral possibilities";
    she is more affirmative. Translating La Fontaine enabled
    her to expand her moral commentary into areas of life in
    which she had little experience. In her late period, she
    reaffirms the values contained in her early work, asserts
    "the need to recognize the unity of spirit with appearance,"
    and meditates "on the need for redemption and ressurrection."
    Excerpted: 1973.4.

10 FURBANK, P. N. "Notes and Queries." <u>The Listener</u>, 72 (29
    October), 683.
    Moore's "art of transition" from concrete to abstract
    through her "serpentine line" and internal rhyme "is one
    of the solid achievements of the century" and can be seen
    in some of the poems of <u>The Arctic Ox</u>. Moore also reflects
    the American culture--its combining dandyism and high seri-
    ousness, its "courtesy towards created things," and its
    "fanatical delicacy...on the subject of money and
    possessions."

1964

11   GARRIGUE, JEAN. "Notes toward a Resemblance: Emily Dickinson,
     Marianne Moore." In Festschrift (1964.33), pp. 52-57.
          Both Moore and Dickinson "have the laconic abruptness of
     decisive daring." Both are readers of the Bible, have "a
     trenchant authority with language," lack "conventional
     smoothness," are original, ask "no threadbare questions,"
     share "a same laughter," are modest, and possess a daring
     wit.

12   GROSS, HARVEY. Sound and Form in Modern Poetry: A Study of
     Prosody from Thomas Hardy to Robert Lowell. Ann Arbor:
     University of Michigan Press, pp. 24, 36-37, 112-17, 230,
     237, 268.
          The emphasis on the visual achieved by Moore's syllabic
     meter is an inheritance from imagism, though the meter it-
     self is more disciplined than the Imagists' free verse.
     "In the Public Garden" has "an almost breathless anecdotal
     rhythm" checked by the syllabics. For Moore, poems are
     like the snakes in "The Monkeys"--"frigid, tense, and sym-
     metrical." But she also accomodates symmetrical form to
     logic and feeling, as she does in "The Labors of Hercules."

13   HAZEL, ROBERT. "A Birthday Cake for Marianne Moore." In Fest-
     schrift (1964.33), pp. 108-109.
          It would be a large cake and a strange party on Moore's
     birthday.

14   HERSEY, JOHN. Comment. In Festschrift (1964.33), p. 135.
          Moore is creatively selfish, making her own "every frag-
     ment of experience" and then giving it back again.

15   HORDER, JOHN. "Right Words, Wrong Words." Spectator, 213 (30
     October), 580.
          Moore's The Arctic Ox is "over-clever." Learning and
     elegance have kept Moore from "important themes."

16   JANSSENS, G. A. "The Dial and the 'Twenties." The Yale Re-
     view, 54 (December), 282-84.
          Joost's Scofield Thayer and The Dial (1964.18) is more
     authoritative than Wasserstrom's The Time of The Dial
     (1963.22). But he "does not satisfactorily answer the
     many detractors of the later Dial" (when Moore was editor).

17   JARRELL, RANDALL. "Fifty Years of American Poetry." In Na-
     tional Poetry Festival Held in the Library of Congress, Oc-
     tober 22-24, 1962, Proceedings. Washington, D.C.: Library
     of Congress, General Reference and Bibliography Division,
     Reference Department, pp. 126-29.
          Reprint of 1963.9.

18   JOOST, NICHOLAS. <u>Scofield Thayer and</u> The Dial: <u>An Illustrated</u>
<u>History</u>. Carbondale: Southern Illinois University Press,
passim.
Moore received the Dial Award for 1924. She became
acting editor on 27 April 1925. In July she became editor.
She offered sympathetic advice to young writers. During
her editorship, she wrote most of the unsigned editorial
comments.

19   KENNEDY, X. J. "The Poet in the Playpen." <u>Poetry</u>, 105 (December), 191-92.
Moore's translations of Perrault's <u>Puss in Boots, The</u>
<u>Sleeping Beauty, & Cinderella</u> are honest and presented in
"handsome English prose."

20   KUNITZ, STANLEY. "Responses, Glosses, Refractions." In <u>Fest-</u>
<u>schrift</u> (1964.33), pp. 77-81.
The town depicted in "The Steeple-Jack" reflects Moore's
values of prudence and hope. "Silence" shows her "passion-
ately fastidious workmanship." Her use of language is
moral in its precision.

21   LEVIN, HARRY. "A Note on Her French Aspect." In <u>Festschrift</u>
(1964.33), pp. 40-43.
Moore has a literary kinship with the French classical
tradition--for example with Moliere, Victor Hugo, Montaigne,
and Buffon. It "led to the most remarkable of her technical
accomplishments, the use of syllabic versification in English," and to essay-like "observations," and, with the
English influence, to a "dual allegiance" to Nature and
Art.

22   LOWELL, ROBERT. Comment. In <u>Festschrift</u> (1964.33), p. 119.
Moore is both "lavish and meticulous" and is equaled by
only one woman poet, Emily Dickinson.

23   McCORD, HOWARD. "Marianne Moore's Chinese Tadpoles." <u>American</u>
<u>Notes and Queries</u>, 3 (September), 5-6.
While the tadpole in "Labors of Hercules" is clearly
analogous to a musical note, in "Novices" the reference to
the "supertadpoles of expression" is enigmatic. It may be
associated, however, with early Chinese written characters,
which resembled and are called "tadpoles."

24   PAYNE, ROBERT. "On Mariamna de Maura." In <u>Festschrift</u>
(1964.33), pp. 21-27.
A fictional biographical and critical study of Moore as
a medieval poet.

1964

25 PLIMPTON, GEORGE. "The World Series with Marianne Moore: Letter from an October Afternoon." Harper's Magazine, 229 (October), 50-58.
An account of attending the second game of the 1963 World Series in Yankee Stadium with Moore (and Robert Lowell). (In the November issue [pp. 91-92], Moore answers questions suggested by Plimpton's essay.)
Reprinted: 1969.19.

26 RAINE, KATHLEEN. "A Letter from Kathleen Raine." In Festschrift (1964.33), pp. 111-12.
I recall two visits with Moore—one after she had been called "the best woman poet in this country," praise that meant nothing to her, she said, since "here in America not more than two, perhaps three, women have ever even tried to write poetry"; the other after the success of Porter's Ship of Fools, which Moore did not finish because she had her "immortal soul to consider." She wrote me a letter asking if I were safe, but I did not know what safety means in Moore's terrible universe.

27 READ, HERBERT. Comment. In Festschrift (1964.33), pp. 28-29.
The "discipline that Miss Moore introduced into Imagism" influenced some of my poems. Her poetry is rococo, formal but free.

28 RICKS, CHRISTOPHER. "Dowager." New Stateman, 68 (16 October), 582.
There are some delightful, whimsical little poems in The Arctic Ox. But many are trivial.

29 ROBSON, JEREMY. "Places, People, Things." The Poetry Review, 55 (Winter), 247.
One can admire the verbal play in Moore's untypical collection The Arctic Ox, but responding fully to the poems is difficult. The notes are irritating. The verse seems imposed on the subjects.

30 ROSS, ALAN. "Daring Old Lady." The London Magazine, NS 4 (December), 91-92.
Moore's poems in Arctic Ox, like those in earlier collections, are jottings made into art by her fastidiousness and instinctive sense of style. Her memory brings together "cultural allusions of widely differing orders."

31 STEPHAN, RUTH. "A Letter for Your Birthday." In Festschrift (1964.33), pp. 82-86.

As a poet, Moore explores the boundary of myth and reality and makes the invisible visible.

32   SWENSON, MAY. "A Matter of Diction." In Festschrift (1964.33),
     pp. 44-49.
        Moore's poetry objectifies "sensual perception and states
     of mind," without being self-conscious. Moore teaches that
     the stuff of poetry is language, not ideas or passions.
     "What Are Years" derives its power from the interplay of
     the consonants s, t and r. The example of Moore annihilates
     the often-made distinction between masculine and feminine
     poetic sensibilities.

33   TAMBIMUTTU, ed. Festschrift for Marianne Moore's Seventy
     Seventh Birthday, by various hands. New York: Tambimuttu
     & Mass, 137 pp.
        Contains a preface by Tambimuttu, titled "Instead of a
     Preface," that comments on the festschrift, his correspon-
     dence with Moore, the precision of her observations and
     diction, and the affinity of her work with Eastern poetry.
     Contains poems about Moore, in her style, or to her by
     Millen Brand, Herbert Cahoon, John Ciardi, Babette Deutsch,
     Richard Eberhart, Eleanor Edelstein, James T. Farrell,
     Allen Ginsberg, David Ignatow, Jeff Kindley, J. Laughlin,
     Nicholas Moore, Howard Moss, Ralph Pomeroy, Robin Skelton,
     William Jay Smith, Vernon Watkins, Robert Penn Warren,
     Theodore Weiss, Carol Weston, and Richard Wilbur. And
     contains essays, letters, and comments: 1964.1-4, 6-8, 11,
     13-14, 20-22, 24, 26-27, 31-32, 34-38, 41, 44.

34   TATE, ALLEN. Comment. In Festschrift (1964.33), p. 113.
        Moore "is spontaneous, elegant, and upright."

35   TODD, RUTHVEN. "With Pencil and Brush." In Festschrift
     (1964.33), pp. 91-92.
        Moore's drawings, like her poetry, record her "love for
     the inescapable, but often unobserved, small details of the
     world."

36   UNTERMEYER, LOUIS. "An Addendum for Marianne Moore." In
     Festschrift (1964.33), pp. 114-15.
        My admiration for Moore constantly grows. She is witty,
     modest, tolerant of experiment, and disdainful of preten-
     tiousness. As a poet she is unique. Her poems are products
     not of craft but of spontaneity. Once I called her poems
     "a kind of witty geometry"; later I said that they were
     fastidious to a fault. Now I think of them "as the ultimate
     in improvisation," combining "the impromptu and the precise."

1964

37   VAN DOREN, MARK. Comment. In <u>Festschrift</u> (1964.33), p. 71.
        As editor of the <u>Dial</u>, Moore asked for revisions in some
     poems I submitted and demonstrated the precise surgery of
     criticism, as well as her generosity.

38   WASSERSTROM, WILLIAM. "Irregular Symmetry: Marianne Moore's
     <u>Dial</u>." In <u>Festschrift</u> (1964.33), pp. 33-37.
        An interview with Moore in 1958 led me to conclude that
     her poetry, her editing of the <u>Dial</u>, and even her Ford cor-
     respondence are based on her desire "to connect high art
     with the general interest."

39   WEATHERHEAD, A. KINGSLEY. "Imagination and Fancy: Robert
     Lowell and Marianne Moore." <u>Texas Studies in Literature
     and Language</u>, 6 (Summer), 188-99.
        Coleridge's distinction between imagination and fancy
     serves to distinguish between two techniques in the handling
     of images by modern American poets. Robert Lowell, espe-
     cially in <u>Lord Weary's Castle</u>, is a poet of imagination.
     The images in his poems are fused by and subordinated to
     idea. Moore is a poet of fancy. Her images are brought
     together by association and are left discrete. In her "St.
     Nicholas," the images of the desired gifts seem at first
     "arbitrarily mustered" but share points of association and,
     by the last stanza, "add up to the poet's request for the
     gift of spiritual conversion."
        Incorporated in 1967.29.

40   _____. "Two Kinds of Vision in Marianne Moore." <u>ELH</u>, 31 (De-
     cember), 482-96.
        Two kinds of vision operate in Moore's poetry: that
     which takes the general view and does not "recognize dis-
     crete particulars" and that which sees particulars and
     "does not subordinate them to a general picture." The
     sentimentality of the first view if often corrected by the
     second, thus revealing Moore's "essential code": "truth
     and feeling must rely on minutely perceived, finite detail."
     The two kinds of vision are contrasted in "The Steeple-
     Jack." The need for close attention to details as a way to
     truth is presented in "The Paper Nautilus." "An Octopus"
     is a sort of voyage among disordinate particulars.
        Incorporated in 1967.29.

41   WHEELER, MONROE. "Reminiscence." In <u>Festschrift</u> (1964.33),
     pp. 127-30.
        I have fond memories of Moore—from my meeting with her
     in the early 1920s, when I published her <u>Marriage</u>, to the
     present.

42 WIDDEMER, MARGARET. "Two Hours with Two Miss Moores." In
    her Golden Friends I Had: Unrevised Memories of Margaret
    Widdemer. Garden City, N.Y.: Doubleday & Co., pp. 314-24.
       Reprint of 1964.43.

43 _____. "Two Hours with Two Miss Moores." Story, 36, no. 142
       (September-October), pp. 52-59.
       An account of a visit with Moore. Among the topics dis-
    cussed were Pound's engagement to H. D. at the University
    of Pennsylvania, Winifred Bryher's generosity, Moore's fans,
    and Moore's mother.

44 YOUNG, MARGUERITE. "An Afternoon with Marianne Moore (1946)."
       In Festschrift (1964.33), pp. 63-66.
       I had an interesting visit with Moore in her Brooklyn
    apartment. She is as experimental as America itself.

                            1965

1   ANON. "American Poetry's Casual Look." The Times (London),
       7 January, p. 13.
          Moore is a "long-honoured" American poet writing in the
    colloquial vein but in a way more refined and fanciful than
    other American poets. The Arctic Ox is not as good as Col-
    lected Poems.

2   ANON. Brief notice of Tambimuttu's Festschrift for Marianne
       Moore's Seventy-Seventh Birthday. The Booklist and Sub-
       scription Books Bulletin, 61 (15 July), 1050.
          The Festschrift provides both an "indirect character
    sketch" and a critique of Moore's work.

3   ANON. "Marianne Moore Wins '65 Poetry Fellowship." The New
       York Times, 3 June, p. 32.
          Moore has been awarded the 1965 fellowship of the Acad-
    emy of American Poets.

4   ANON. "Notes Etc. on Books Etc." The Carleton Miscellany,
       6 (Fall), 216.
          The Festschrift (1964.33) is "uneven."

5   ANON. "Poetry Puts Ox to Rights." The Times Literary Supple-
       ment, no. 3,289 (11 March), p. 196.
          In the Arctic Ox Moore continues to write "the level,
    discriminating tone, the mischievously specific eye, the
    brave refusal of solemnity."

1965

6   CASEY, FLORENCE. "New Paperbacks." The Christian Science
     Monitor, Eastern edition, 15 April, p. 11.
        The highpoint of A Marianne Moore Reader is the poetry;
     the low is the collection of reviews.

7   CONNOLLY, CYRIL. "Marianne Moore." In his The Modern Move-
     ment: One Hundred Key Books from England, France and Amer-
     ica, 1880-1950. London: A Grafton Book, Andre Deutsch and
     Hamish Hamilton, pp. 76-77.
        Moore's Selected Poems is one of the key books of the
     Modern Movement, in which Moore is "an imperceptible vita-
     min of little-known properties whose absence could prove
     terminal."

8   DODSWORTH, MARTIN. "The Secrecy of Marianne Moore." The Re-
     view, no. 15 (April), pp. 18-25.
        Moore is a surprisingly private poet in the supposedly
     "open" American society. Although her poems are direct,
     honest, in "moralizing comment" and although she praises
     simplicity, Moore's style is complex, making use of anti-
     poetic rhythms and intricate stanzas. The conflict between
     content and style could be explained as Moore's eccentric-
     ity, an explanation that implies an aestheticism at odds
     with the moral statements made in such poems as "Novices."
     But her best work is "simply and directly expressive,"
     often dealing with the defenses of animals against an un-
     friendly nature and with man's lack of humility, the best
     defense. Moore's style, including her use of quotation
     marks, is at once her attempt at humility and a means of
     attracting the reader. Although the more public poems of
     Arctic Ox tend toward sentimentality, her style has changed
     little.
        Reprinted: 1968.19.

9   DUNCAN, ROBERT. "The Lasting Contribution of Ezra Pound."
     Agenda, 4 (October-November), 23-26.
        Pound's poetry differs from Moore's and from the pre-1949
     Williams' in taking the rhythmic phrase rather than a fixed
     number of syllables as its base. Moore's syllabic verse is
     one of the "by-ways in the evolution of American poetics."

10 GARRIGUE, JEAN. Marianne Moore. University of Minnesota
     Pamphlets on American Writers, no. 50. Minneapolis: Uni-
     versity of Minnesota, 48 pp.
        Critics and poets have not neglected Moore's idiosyncra-
     tic poetry, which has also received the recognition of of-
     ficialdom. Her Observations presents a new voice in modern

poetry--one that speaks in prose rhythms and avoids poetic diction--and uses "a new subject matter" that arises from Moore's strong moral convictions rather than from any disillusionment. Her method includes the use of notes, quotation, hidden rhyme, syllabic measure, and "juxtaposition of incongruities." After <u>Observations,</u> her poetry becomes more subtly musical, more fantastic and humorous, more concerned with animals, and less ironic and satirical.
    Reprinted with additions: 1971.6, 1974.3. Excerpted: 1973.4.

11   HALL, DONALD. "An Interview with Donald Hall." <u>McCall's</u>, 93 (December), 74, 182-86, 188-90.
    A largely biographical interview--about Moore's relationship with her mother, her attitude toward marriage, school, living in Brooklyn, religion, a visit with Eliot, travel, baseball, boxing, food, circus, reading, Edith Sitwell, health, favorite poems.

12   HAMMEL, LISA. "Marianne Moore Takes Poetic License by Modeling in Sidewalk Hat Show." <u>The New York Times</u>, 13 July, p. 24.
    Wearing a black velvet tricorn hat, Moore served as a model for a sidewalk showing of hats by Maskal, Inc.

13   JENNINGS, ELIZABETH. "Idea and Expression in Emily Dickinson, Marianne Moore, and Ezra Pound." In <u>American Poetry</u>. Edited by Irvin Ehrenpreis. Stratford-upon-Avon Studies, 7. New York: St. Martin's Press, pp. 102-106.
    Moore's main interest is moral, not esthetic or social. She uses the apparent bric-a-brac in her poems "to tell a story or illustrate a theme." There is emotion in her poems, but it is controlled. Her poems are carefully designed patterns.

14   KENNER, HUGH. "The Experience of the Eye: Marianne Moore's Tradition." <u>The Southern Review</u>, NS 1 (Autumn), 754-69.
    Sometimes seen as merely eccentric or peripheral, Moore actually belongs in the tradition "of describing accurately the thing seen." Moore's discovery--the influence of the typewriter is evident--was that the animals or objects of her poems "exist only on the page." As in "The Fish," she uses syllabics, spatial arrangements, optical puns, unusual syntax, and quotations to stress the visual and therefore objective being of her words and poems. Her poems are "systems" rather than utterances, and these systems, as in "An Octopus," usually have as their subjects other "self-sufficient systems of energy" (animals, moving glacier, and

1965

so forth) that, like her poems, "can appropriate...almost
anything that comes near." Since her poems enact with rigor
"the moral virtues they celebrate," Moore escapes the dandy-
ism seen in such writers as Hemingway who view their descriptions as feats rather than homages.
Reprinted: 1970.10. Revised: 1975.6. Excerpted:
1975.2.

15 LUNDY, GERALD. "Blessing and Felicitous Dragon." Northwest
Review, 7 (Spring-Summer), 94.
Moore is a magpie, a meadowlark. Her Marianne Moore
Reader, now in a Compass Books edition, is worth the price.

16 O'CONNELL, MARGARET F. "Yuletide for Young Readers." The New
York Times Book Review, 5 December, p. 60.
The revised edition of Rock Crystal is "an event for
rejoicing for literate families."

17 PAIGE, NANCY. "Christmas Books 1965." Library Journal, 90
(15 October), 4531.
Rock Crystal, out of print since 1954, is now reissued
by Pantheon.

18 SERGEANT, HOWARD. "Poetry Review." English, 15 (Spring), 154.
Moore is one of the few poets who have exerted a definite
influence on modern poetry. Arctic Ox shows the wide range
of her knowledge but contains many trivial poems.

19 SIMONDS, C. H. "Books in Brief." National Review, 17 (7 September), 785.
The Festschrift (1964.33) is "dismal," filled for the
most part with "trifling reminiscences" that are focused
not on Moore but on the "psyches and petty concerns" of the
contributors.

20 SMITH, WILLIAM JAY. "New Books of Poems: From Last August to
This." Harper's Magazine, 231 (August), 108.
In the Festschrift (1964.33) are tributes to Moore by
Monroe Wheeler, who praises her originality, and Auden, who
acknowledges his debt. Auden's About the House shows this
debt to Moore, or perhaps his common ancestry with her.

1966

1 ANON. "Books--Authors. Marianne Moore Picks a Winner." The
New York Times, 9 December, p. 44.

Moore selected from a hat the name of the publisher who
will be granted $55,000 by the National Foundation of the
Arts and Humanities to publish an anthology of works from
little magazines.

2 ANON. "Miss Moore in Manhattan." The New Yorker, 41 (29 January), 25-26.
Moore recently moved from Brooklyn to Manhattan. She
had lived in Brooklyn for thirty-six years but feels it is
no longer safe. We visited her new apartment.

3 ANON. Review of Tell Me, Tell Me. The Virginia Kirkus Service,
34 (15 July), 748.
Moore's later style is characterized by a "terrible pre-
dictability." She is now "indulging herself," displaying
an eccentricity that is "no longer stimulating" but is "a
highly private, cultivated dottiness, stuffed with apho-
ristic jugglery, and unredeemed by pyrotechnical skill."

4 ASHBERY, JOHN. "Jerboas, Pelicans, and Pee Wee Reese." New
York World Journal Tribune Book Week, 4 (30 October), 1, 8.
Moore is possibly "the greatest living poet in English."
Tell Me, Tell Me is "her longest and best collection since
the 1935 Selected Poems." There is a new clarity in her
work, perhaps the result of translating La Fontaine.

5 BURKE, HERBERT C. Biref notice of Tell Me, Tell Me. Library
Journal, 91 (1 September), 3961.
Tell Me, Tell Me is "a delight" that belongs in all po-
etry collections.

6 DEMBO, L. S. "Marianne Moore: Unparticularities." In his
Conceptions of Reality in Modern American Poetry. Berkeley
and Los Angeles: University of California Press, pp. 108-17.
Like Stevens and Williams, Moore is a radical aestheti-
cist and objectivist. For her, the ideal mind is one that
is able to avoid egoism and sentiment (to achieve a moral
integrity) and thus is able to see and express the unparticularities behind particularities. Her position is il-
lustrated or implied by "He 'Digesteth Harde Yron,'" "By
Disposition of Angels," "Armor's Undermining Modesty," "The
Mind Is an Enchanting Thing," "The Hero," "A Carriage from
Sweden," "An Octopus," and other poems.

7 DICKEY, JAMES. "What the Angels Missed." The New York Times
Book Review, 25 December, pp. 1, 16.

1966

If I had to choose a poet to construct heaven, I would choose Moore, who "has spent her life in remaking--or making--our world from particulars that we have never adequately understood on our own." Her heaven would be "a realm of Facts" and "joyous conjunctions." Tell Me, Tell Me does not reveal a new phase, just a deeper use of her one phase.

8   ENGEL, BERNARD. "A Democratic Vista of Religion." The Georgia Review, 20 (Spring), 84-89.
     Moore, Williams, and Stevens share an "insistence upon the central importance of religious questions" and the exploration of them in literature. Many of Moore's poems celebrate "fortitude" and "'discipline' of spirit."

9   ETTER, DAVE. "New Slants of Light." Chicago Tribune Books Today, 3 (20 November), p. 13
     Tell Me, Tell Me is one of Moore's "finest efforts, full of her characteristic generosity, innocence, and wisdom." Often charged with obscurity, Moore has now achieved more clarity, at no cost.

10   FOWLER, ALBERT. "That I May Yet Recover." Fellowship, 32 (March), 5-6.
     Moore's "In Distrust of Merits" has an important message for today. She knew that the real struggle is not external.

11   FRIENDLY, ALFRED. "Poets Take over U.S. Happening. Delegates Join Marianne Moore at Goldbergs'." The New York Times, 10 June, p. 24.
     Moore was the guest of honor at a party given by Mrs. Arthur J. Goldberg. She and other poets and guests read some poetry.

12   GOODWIN, K. L. "Five Important Poets." In his The Influence of Ezra Pound. London: Oxford University Press, pp. 157-64.
     Pound's influence on Moore can be seen in her use of the imagistic and ideogrammic methods, use of quotations, and admission of the wide variety of experience as the material of poetry. She made possible the longer imagistic poem by her "image-within-image construction," which is seen, for example, in "A Grave," a poem that also shows her use of abstract terms to control images. She uses her version of the ideogrammic method in "The Frigate Pelican," "Style," and "Critics and Connoisseurs." Moore's use of quotations differs from Pound's and Eliot's in that the quotations do not become part of her subject and their sources are irrelevant.

94

1966

13 HOWES, BARBARA. "Miss Moore Herself." The New Republic, 155
    (17 December), 31.
        The title of Tell Me, Tell Me recalls Joyce's "tell me,
    tell me, elm" in Finnegans Wake. Its poems show the broad
    range of Moore's interests. They enrich us.

14 HYMAN, STANLEY EDGAR. "Marianne Moore at Seventy-Four." In
    his Standards: A Chronicle of Books for Our Time. New
    York: Horizon Press, pp. 38-42.
        Reprint of 1961.10.

15 LASK, THOMAS. "Books of the Times." The New York Times, 6
    December, p. 45.
        Through the alchemy of her "personal logic," Moore makes
    poems out of juxtaposed "phrases, ideas, images." The po-
    ems of Tell Me, Tell Me seem a kind of "shorthand."

16 _____. "Writers Discuss Status of Poetry." The New York Times,
    1 December, p. 57.
        Moore, Robert Graves, Stanley Kunitz, and Howard Nemerov
    conducted a symposium on "Poetry—For Whom?" at the New
    School.

17 MADDOCKS, MELVIN. "She Has Iron in Her Writing." The Chris-
    tian Science Monitor, 17 November, p. 15.
        Behind the "charming disarray" in Tell Me, Tell Me is
    "an iron firmness."

18 MILES, JOSEPHINE. "Moore: 'Spenser's Ireland.'" In Master
    Poems of the English Language: Over One Hundred Poems To-
    gether with Introductions by Leading Poets and Critics of
    the English-Speaking World. Edited by Oscar Williams. New
    York: Trident Press, pp. 938-41.
        The stanzas of "Spenser's Ireland" enumerate the contra-
    dictory "traits and beliefs" of Ireland. They are unified
    by an interweaving of statement, sound, and meter. Part of
    the meaning of the poem is hidden in the allusion to Spenser,
    whose View of the Present State of Ireland, like Moore's
    poem, follows the "principle of inner dialogue."

19 PARKIN, REBECCA PRICE. "Certain Difficulties in Reading Mari-
    anne Moore: Exemplified in Her 'Apparition of Splendor.'"
    PMLA, 81 (June), 167-72.
        Understatement, indirection, economy of image, use of
    animals to subsume abstraction, and other characteristics
    make Moore's poetry difficult, as resistant as the porcupine

1966

in "Apparition of Splendor." Through the juxtaposition of Dürer's rhinoceros, an eighteenth-century fairy tale, and an implied analogy between porcupines and a Downeaster, this poem presents its theme of assertion-through-abnegation.

20 ____. "Some Characteristics of Marianne Moore's Humor." College English, 27 (February), 403-408.
Moore's humor amuses and teaches. It arises from unexpected juxtapositions, equations, hierarchies, and repetition. Humor in "The Pangolin" serves as a sign of "grace," that is, the maintenance of poise before "the basic absurdity...of the human situation." "O to Be a Dragon," "Apparition of Splendor," "No Swan So Fine," "Then the Ermine," "Tell Me, Tell Me" are also characteristic.

21 RUKEYSER, MURIEL. "A Crystal for the Metaphysical." Saturday Review, 49 (1 October), 52-53, 81.
The poems in Tell Me, Tell Me are notable for their strength and form. During my recent visit with Moore, we discussed her plan to write her memoirs, her affection for such poets as Robert Francis and Elizabeth Bishop, her dislike of "In Distrust of Merits" because of its didacticism, and other topics. Moore makes poems in which the edges of things, including the written word, are juxtaposed, forced to meet.

22 STERN, MICHAEL. "Brooklyn Loses Marianne Moore." The New York Times, 20 January, p. 37.
Not feeling safe in the Brooklyn apartment in which she had lived since 1929, Moore has moved to an apartment in the Village. Bums and drunks would ring her doorbell at odd hours; her neighbors were robbed.

23 STEVENS, WALLACE. Letters of Wallace Stevens. Edited by Holly Stevens. New York: Alfred A Knopf, passim.
Includes five letters to Moore and numerous references to her, including references to her as a better poet than Williams and to Stevens' review of Moore (1935.20), in which he meant to say "scrupulous" rather than "fastidious."

24 WILLIAMS, WILLIAM CARLOS. "Marianne Moore." In The William Carlos Williams Reader. Edited by M. L. Rosenthal. New York: New Directions, pp. 384-93.
Reprint of 1925.20.

1967

1 ANON. "Books in Brief." The Beloit Poetry Journal, 17 (Summer), 34.
   Tell Me, Tell Me is a fine collection on an "amazing variety of subjects."

2 ANON. Brief notice of Tell Me, Tell Me. The Booklist and Subscription Books Bulletin, 63 (1 February), 559-60.
   The poems reveal Moore's "customary preoccupation with life's versatility and vigor" and her precise style and use of apt quotation.

3 ANON. "Forecasts." Publishers' Weekly, 192 (2 October), 52.
   Moore's Complete Poems is forecast for publication on 15 November.

4 ANON. "MacDowell Colony, 50 Years Old, Hails Marianne Moore." The New York Times, 21 August, p. 29.
   Moore was awarded today the MacDowell Medal at MacDowell Colony.

5 ANON. "N.Y.U. Graduates Warned on Rigid War Attitudes." The New York Times, 14 June, p. 36.
   Moore was awarded an honorary Doctor of Letters degree by New York University yesterday.

6 ANON. "Poet of the Tricorn." The New York Times, 14 April, p. 36.
   Moore, honored last night by the Poetry Society of America, is beloved for her wit as well as her looks. She has won many awards. She is a baseball fan.

7 ANON. Review of Tell Me, Tell Me. Choice, 4 (November), 984.
   The book belongs in every library.

8 ANON. "This Week." The Christian Century, 84 (15 November), 1468.
   If we could "canonize just one living poet," it would be Moore. Complete Poems is her canon.

9 ASHBERY, JOHN. "Straight Lines over Rough Terrain." The New York Times Book Review, 26 November, pp. 1, 42.
   After reading Complete Poems, I am tempted to call Moore "our greatest modern poet." She is underestimated. She is not a "Mary Poppins of poetry" or "an American La Fontaine." She is "a poet writing on many levels at once to produce

work of an irreducible symphonic texture." Her poems begin simply but become complex. In "An Octopus" and in her translations of La Fontaine, we see "her gift for language-making."

10 AUDEN, W. H. "A Mosaic for Marianne Moore." New York Review of Books, 9 (9 November), p. 3.
    Poem.
    Reprinted: 1969.2, 1969.3.

11 BRANNUM, MARY, and the editors. "Marianne Moore." In When I Was Sixteen. New York: Platt & Munk, pp. 218-21.
    Provides a brief biographical sketch, characterizing Moore as "unfrivolous" and "less eccentric than direct" and her poetry as attentive "to the particular." The sketch is followed by Moore's answers to questions about her life and interests (pp. 223-31).

12 CUSHMAN, JEROME. Review of Complete Poems. Library Journal, 92 (15 October), 3647.
    Moore dislikes "prettified poetry." Within her "cryptic restraint," there is a subtle didacticism. This book is recommended "for high school, public, and academic libraries."

13 DAVIS, DOUGLAS M. "In the Flow of Poetry, the Ladies Flourish." The National Observer, 6 (6 February), 31.
    Tell Me, Tell Me is conventional and academic.

14 DONOGHUE, DENIS. "Moorish Gorgeousness." The New York Review of Books, 7 (12 January), 3-4.
    Moore is a poet of observation and of relations between appearances. She uses her own and others' observations. The poems of Tell Me, Tell Me imply that "anything is poetic" if one is attentive. Moore does not seek absolutes, though she has her private sense of them. See seeks instead precision in the use of words, as her revision of "Sun" indicates. Moreover, she writes with grace and good manners.
    Reprinted and expanded: 1968.21 and 1969.28.

15 ELLIOTT, GEORGE P. "Poetry Chronicle." The Hudson Review, 20 (Spring), 139-40.
    In Tell Me, Tell Me Moore's "manner has turned into mannerism, and her optimism has become extensive."

16 FULLER, EDMUND. "Quartet of Masters Tops Big Poetry Crop." The Wall Street Journal, 170 (27 December), 8.
    Moore's incomplete Complete Poems reveals her playful spirit.

1967

17 GARRIGUE, JEAN. "Gaiety in Finished Form." New Leader, 50
(4 December), 23-24.
For Complete Poems, Moore has revised, mostly by exclusion of lines, thirteen of her earlier poems. Others are
omitted entirely. The revisions take some getting used to.
Moore's early and recent poetry displays her "remarkable
sense of detail." Some recent poems, such as "Blue Bug,"
suggest "Moore's interest in a new kind of lightness and
grace," and some suffer from being "too open, probably too
public."

18 GILROY, HARRY. "Marianne Moore Steps out Tonight in Beloved
New York on Birthday No. 80." The New York Times, 15 November, p. 42.
Moore will celebrate her eightieth birthday today.
During an interview, she called attention to her "In Distrust of Merits," confessed that she once hoped for a
writing job with the Boston Evening Transcript, and discussed other topics. She will celebrate tonight with
Monroe Wheeler, Glenway Wescott, and her brother.

19 _____. "Marianne Moore Wins Gold Medal." The New York Times,
14 April, p. 36.
The Poetry Society of America last night presented its
Gold Medal for Distinguished Achievement to Moore. Mayor
Lindsay called her the poet laureate of New York City.
Robert Lowell called her "the best woman poet in English."
And Langston Hughes called her "the most famous Negro woman
poet in America."

20 HOCHMAN, SANDRA. "Marianne Moore's Magic." The Nation, 204
(8 May), 602.
Moore's art in Tell Me, Tell Me is not mere observation.
Moore discovers the "musical possibilities locked within
our common speech."

22 HOFFMAN, DANIEL. "Two Ladies of Legend." The Reporter, 37
(28 December), 41-43.
Although she never wrote the ambitious long poem and although comparing Complete Poems with Poems shows that she
"began writing at the top of her form," Moore is one who
altered the language, forms, and feelings of American poetry.
And beneath her modernity is a spiritual quality of an older
tradition.

22 HOWARD, JANE. "Leading Lady of U. S. Verse." Life, 62 (13
January), 37-38.

1967

As was obvious at a party celebrating the publication of
Tell Me, Tell Me, Moore "springs from the genus of spry,
Darling Little Old Ladies." She is known more for her
spryness than for her poetry. Spry and darling as she is,
her poetry is complex--"rich and energetic but obscure,
virginal and mathematical...unjuicy." She never married.
Her talk is wide-ranging. People fuss over her.

23 JOOST, NICHOLAS. The Dial: Years of Transition, 1912-1920.
    Barre, Mass.: Barre Publishers, pp. 125, 151, 168, 170,
    171, 230, 256, 272-73.
        The preoccupation of Scofield Thayer, James Sibley Watson,
    and Moore with the work of art as a piece of polished utter-
    ance found expression in their editorial judgments and
    caused the Dial to be respected and detested.

24 KENNER, HUGH. "Artemis and Harlequin." National Review, 19
    (26 December), 1432-33.
        Critics have called Moore "the greatest living observer"
    and have remarked on her "idiosyncratic clipping-file" but
    otherwise have not had much to say. It she battles critics,
    she must be "the bibliographers' despair." In Complete Po-
    ems the metamorphosis of "Poetry" ends in a three-line poem.
    Moore's toads are often verbal--quotations--and the point
    of her poems is "the arrowy motion of the mind through
    them."

25 LEWIS, R. W. B. The Poetry of Hart Crane: A Critical Study.
    Princeton University Press, pp. 120, 187, 188, 192.
        As editor of the Dial, Moore rejected Crane's "Passage."
    And she "dismembered" his "Wine Menagerie," a poem that
    "envisages the dismemberment of several males by several
    females."

26 MADDOCKS, MELVIN. "Matching the Lady and the Poet." The
    Christian Science Monitor, 16 November, p. 15.
        The "large non-poetry-reading public" has transferred to
    Moore the personal affection it had for Robert Frost. She
    is thought of as a "Victorian aunt." Her poetry, in Com-
    plete Poems, is complex, sometimes leaving a reader with
    not an insight but a "glowing feeling that one has had an
    insight."

27 MARTZ, LOUIS. "Recent Poetry: Fruits of a Renaissance." The
    Yale Review, 56 (June), 597-98.
        The best poem in Tell Me, Tell Me is "Baseball and
    Writing."

28 ROCKETT, WILLIAM. Review of Tell Me, Tell Me. The Canadian
Forum, 47 (June), 69.
This collection is a confused mixture of intended and
unintended aburdities. It often treats the commonplace as
if it is sublime. "Dream" is a good poem, though.

29 WEATHERHEAD, A. KINGSLEY. The Edge of the Image: Marianne
Moore, William Carlos Williams, and Some Other Poets.
Seattle and London: University of Washington Press, xiv,
251 pp. (See especially pp. 39-42, 58-95.)
Like Williams, Moore is a poet of the faculty Coleridge
termed the fancy. Unlike poets of the imagination (such as
Lowell and Stevens) who fuse and subordinate to ideas the
images in their poems, Moore keeps her images discrete,
seemingly presented for their own sake. Moore's "Saint
Nicholas" is an example of her technique. She expresses
feeling by "concrete images" that are "carefully perceived."
She has two kinds of Vision (seen, for example, in "The
Steeple-Jack"): the long view that "presents a general
panorama" rather than particulars and the close view that
presents particulars not subordinated to "a general picture."
Her poetic practice can be seen in "The Paper Nautilus,"
"An Octopus," "A Grave," "Tom Fool at Jamaica," "England,"
"He 'Digesteth Harde Yron,'" "In Distrust of Merits,"
"Leonardo da Vinci's," "In the Public Garden," and "Silence."
The multiplication of fanciful images serves to restrain
feeling and sentimentality and thus implies feeling in the
act of escaping from it. Moore's use of quotations and
statements often resembles her use of images: they too are
treated as items "from the heterogeneous objective world."
Her use of form and sound patterns to contribute to meaning
and to unify diverse images is seen in "The Pangolin," "The
Jerboa," and "An Egyptian Pulled Glass Bottle in the Shape
of a Fish."
Incorporates 1964.39, 1964.40. Excerpted: 1975.2.

30 WHITMAN, ALDEN. "Marianne Moore and Voznesensky Meet on Mayor's
Lawn." The New York Times, 14 May, p. 85.
Moore met with Soviet poet Voznesensky at Gracie Mansion
yesterday.

31 ZITNER, S. P. "Urgency and Deference." Poetry, 110 (September), 423-24.
Tell Me, Tell Me shows that Moore's sensibility endures.
Moore does not exclude areas of experience often avoided in
contemporary poetry.

1968

1   ANON. "Book Award Given to Marianne Moore." The New York
    Times, 11 December, p. 45.
        Yesterday Moore was awarded the National Medal for Lit-
    erature by the National Book Committee.

2   ANON. Brief notice of Complete Poems. The Booklist and Sub-
    scription Books Bulletin, 64 (15 February), 674, 683.
        Complete Poems gathers some old poems and adds some new.

3   ANON. "Illustration." The New York Times, 11 April, p. 1.
        Moore tossed out the first ball to open the season at
    Yankee Stadium yesterday.

4   ANON. "Lead-Off Lady." Newsweek, 71 (22 April), 59.
        Moore threw out the first ball on opening day at Yankee
    Stadium.

5   ANON. "Marianne (Craig) Moore." Current Biography, 29 (April),
    26-29.
        Updates and expands the biographical sketch of 1952.9.

6   ANON. "Marianne Moore at 81 Wins National Medal." Library
    Journal, 93 (1 December), 4481.
        Moore has won the 1968 National Medal for Literature.

7   ANON. "Marianne Moore Awarded National Medal." National Book
    Committee Quarterly, 7 (December), 2.
        On 15 November Moore was named winner of the 1968 Nation-
    al Medal for Literature. She is the fourth American and
    first woman to receive the award, which was presented to
    her on 10 December.

8   ANON. "Marianne Moore Receives National Medal for Literature."
    Publishers' Weekly, 194 (18 November), 60.
        Moore has won the 1968 National Medal for Literature.

9   ANON. "Notes Etc on Books Etc." The Carleton Miscellany, 9
    (Summer), 116.
        Moore has done some editing in Complete Poems.

10 ANON. "People." Time, 91 (19 April), 43.
        At Yankee Stadium Moore threw out, to catcher Frank
    Fernandez, the first ball of the 1968 season. She kept her
    pitch low.

1968

11 ANON. "Princeton Gives Degrees to 756." The New York Times,
12 June, p. 19.
Moore was awarded an honorary Doctor of Letters degree
today by Princeton University.

12 ANON. Review of Complete Poems. Choice, 4 (February), 1382.
Complete Poems is not a definitive edition but belongs
in every library.

13 ANON. "Worker's Compensation." Newsweek, 72 (25 November),
60.
Hearing the National Book Committee's tribute to her poetry as something that evokes "enchanted glimpses of eter-
nity," Moore replied: "Indeed! That's a big claim. I'm
not Columbus discovering America, you know. I'm a worker
working with words, that's all."

14 BOGAN, LOUISE. "Books: Verse." The New Yorker, 44 (30
March), 137.
Complete Poems has little new work.

15 BURKE, KENNETH. "Motives and Motifs in the Poetry of Marianne
Moore." In Modern Poetry: Essays in Criticism. Edited by
John Hollander. London: Oxford University Press, pp.
201-18.
Reprint of 1942.2.

16 BURNS, GERALD. "Poets and Anthologies." Southwest Review, 53
(Summer), 332.
In Complete Poems, Moore has reduced "Poetry" to three
lines but is still "a pack rat" whose work is "full of
found objects." She uses light rhymes to create "demi-
pauses" which play "against cadenced Bryn Mawr."

17 DEMBO, L. S. Review of Weatherhead's Edge of the Image
(1967.29). American Literature, 40 (November), 419.
Despite the ambiguity of Coleridge's concepts of imagination and fancy, Weatherhead usefully applies them in contrasting poetry, like Moore's, in which images retain their
integrity and poetry in which images blur as they become
subordinate to an organic structure.

18 DICKEY, JAMES. "Marianne Moore." In his Babel to Byzantium:
Poets & Poetry Now. New York: Farrar, Straus and Giroux,
pp. 156-64.
Reprint of 1962.8 and 1966.7.

1968

19   DODSWORTH, MARTIN. "Marianne Moore." In his The Modern Poet:
     Essays from The Review. Edited by Ian Hamilton. London:
     MacDonald, pp. 125.33.
            Reprint of 1965.8.

20   _____. "Towards the Baseball Poem." The Listener, 79 (27
     June), 842.
            American poets like James Dickey, Robert Bly, Theodore
     Roethke, and Alan Dugan seem at times too much concerned
     with writing "Literature" rather than poetry. They like
     symbols more than life, tokens of excellence more than the
     "reality which in fact creates that excellence." Moore is
     a contrast. She has been "fighting for poetry against Lit-
     erature for many years."

21   DONOGHUE, DENIS. "The Proper Plenitude of Fact." In his The
     Ordinary Universe: Soundings in Modern Literature. New
     York: The Macmillan Co., pp. 42-50.
            Expanded version of 1967.14. Excerpted: 1974.2, 1976.1.

22   FAIRCHILD, HOXIE NEALE. Religious Trends in English Poetry.
     Vol. 6: 1920-1965: Valley of Dry Bones. New York: Co-
     lumbia University Press, pp. 40, 44-46, 189, 192, 217-18,
     224, 452-53.
            Granddaughter of a Presbyterian minister and herself a
     Presbyterian, Moore writes poems that show a "healthy moral
     sense" that "is rooted in religion." She is a Christian poet
     because of her delight in the "creations of God's world."

23   FAUCHEREAU, SERGE. "Les avatars de l'imagisme: Marianne Moore,
     Hart Crane." In his Lecture de la poésie américaine. Col-
     lection Critique. [Paris]: Les éditions de minuit, pp.
     97-100.
            Moore was on the fringe of imagism in her regard for ob-
     jects but not in her prosody, which is syllabic rather than
     free or accentual. Her experiments in rhyme show, perhaps,
     the influence of Provençal poetry. She seems to regard her
     art as a game in which she plays with words. Although her
     poetry considers itself minor, its influence is great.

24   FOSS, LAURENCE. "Miss Moore." The Christian Century, 85 (8
     May), 611.
            Poem.

25   FULLER, ROY. "Poetry in My Time." The Listener, 79 (27 June),
     834.
            Auden seems "to have assumed the Moorish style in 1939,
     with the poem 'In the Memory of Sigmund Freud.'" Since
     then, he has made frequent use of syllabic meter.

26   [FULLER, ROY B.] "Virtuoso Fiddling: Marianne Moore's Syl-
      labics." The Times Literary Supplement, no. 3457 (30 May),
      552.
         Complete Poems is incomplete, and Moore's literary ante-
      cedents, especially for her syllabics, are not at all clear.
      Moore writes "poetry with prose's rhetoric, complexity and
      ease." When she recites, she pays no heed to line endings.
      Her rhyme and meter serve to "delay and enrich" sense and
      feeling. Her influence can be seen in Auden. In her later
      poetry there is more New Yorker cosiness. Moore's work on
      La Fontaine unfortunately diverted her talents from her own
      poetry. It is now clear that she has written "a quite sub-
      stantial number of brilliant and wholly successful poems."
         Reprinted: 1969.9. Expanded in 1971.5.

27   GILROY, HARRY. "Marianne Moore, 81 Today, Given Literature
      Medal." The New York Times, 15 November, p. 44.
         Moore has been awarded the National Medal for Literature.

28   GRANT, DAMIAN. "Centre Court." The Tablet, 222 (6 July),
      673-74.
         Complete Poems "puzzles, excites, rewards."

29   HECHT, ANTHONY. "Writers' Rights and Readers' Rights." The
      Hudson Review, 21 (Spring), 207-209.
         In Complete Poems Moore omits and revises radically and
      mercilessly. I regret her not having been more sparing,
      since her work exhibits "a mind of great fastidiousness, a
      delicate and cunning moral sensibility, a tact, a decorum,
      a rectitude, and finally and most movingly, a capacity for
      pure praise that has absolutely biblical awe in it."

30   JANSSENS, G. A. M. The American Literary Review: A Critical
      History. The Hague: Mouton, pp. 33-34, 44, 51, 53, 57,
      67, 74, 78, 82, 84-89.
         It was the policy of the Dial rather than Moore's work
      as editor that was attacked during her editorship. The
      affair of Crane's "Wine Menagerie" has been made too much
      of.

31   [MARSDEN, H. J.] "Precisie en te veel details." De Gids, 131,
      no. 9-10, 297-300. Signed "J. Bernlef."
         At its best, Moore's poetry strikes a balance between her
      sometimes conflicting preferences for lucidity and precision.
      The long versions of "Poetry" show what can be gained from
      precision; the short versions sacrifice precision to lucid-
      ity and thus are failures of the imagination. The short
      version of "The Steeple-Jack" shows what can be gained from

1968

> lucidity; the long version lacks intensity because of the
> confusing proliferation of precisely listed details.

32   MORSE, SAMUEL FRENCH. "Poetry 1966." <u>Contemporary Literature</u>,
     9 (Winter), 115.
     <u>Tell Me, Tell Me</u> has Moore's customary individuality but
     also an "increasing spareness and moral focus."

33   PETSCHEK, WILLA. "Poet for the Brooklyn Dodgers." <u>Manchester</u>
     <u>Guardian</u>, 28 February, p. 9.
     Moore is direct as a person but indirect in poetry,
     writing something like "a Bach fugue." Her apartment is
     crowded with books and other objects.

34   REED, REX. "Marianne Moore: Autumn, 1966." In his <u>Do You</u>
     <u>Sleep in the Nude?</u> New York: The New American Library,
     pp. 124-28.
     This autumn Moore will narrate a performance of
     Stravinsky's <u>The Flood</u>. She lives in Greenwich Village.
     Her apartment is cluttered. Moore commented on her life
     and writing during my visit.

35   SEYMOUR-SMITH, MARTIN. "In Lieu of the Lyre." <u>Spectator</u>, 220
     (10 May), 634.
     Moore is "the most impersonal" of poets. Disliking the
     rawness of poetry's raw material, she excludes what she
     cannot honestly admit. Crane's shrewd observation that
     Moore's extreme detachment seems "a kind of inspiration"
     agrees in part with Moore's statement that her poetry was
     poetry only because of the lack of another category in which
     to place it. She produces "true poetry from an astonish-
     ingly narrow range of experience."

36   SMITH, WILLIAM J. "A Place for the Genuine." <u>The New Republic</u>,
     158 (24 February), 34, 36.
     All of Moore's poetry is a sort of translation--from
     observation and emotion. <u>Complete Poems</u> cuts lines, omits
     poems, restores poems. The most puzzling cut reduces "Po-
     etry" from an essay to an epigram, one that serves "as a
     kind of coda" to the volume and Moore's career. In revising,
     Moore has not hesitated to loosen her syllabics. If her own
     poems are precise, her translations of La Fontaine are
     confused.

37   STERN, MICHAEL. "Marianne Moore Preaches Gently against War."
     <u>The New York Times</u>, 20 June, p. 47.
     Moore recited yesterday at a poetry reading sponsored
     by the New York Parks Department. Among the poems she read
     was "In Distrust of Merits."

38 SYMONS, JULIAN. "New Poetry." Punch, 254 (19 June), 902.
    The value of Moore's poetry of "quirky comparisons" has
    been exaggerated. Complete Poems is the product of "a cul-
    tivated intelligence."

39 THWAITE, ANTHONY. "Guts, Brain, Nerves." New Statesman, 75
    (17 May), 659.
    Just as Theodore Roethke writes from the guts and John
    Berryman from the nerves, Moore writes from the brain. The
    author of Complete Poems seems a "Grandma Moses with a summa
    cum laude from Bryn Mawr."

40 TOMLINSON, CHARLES. "Marianne Moore: Her Poetry and Her Crit-
    ics." Agenda, 6 (Autumn-Winter), 137-42.
    Although earlier American poets used syllabic meter,
    Moore used it more audaciously, incorporating prose and al-
    lowing "great variation of line length and unpredictability
    of rhythmic pattern." Moore's originality is also attribu-
    table to her close observation of objects, a feature that
    allies her with Pound and Williams. Criticism of Moore has
    been either rigorous and "clear minded" or sentimental. She
    may have "suffered more from lax adulation than almost any
    other significant poet of our century." While early in her
    career Moore's poetry was regarded as arid and restrained
    in feeling, it is now called human, warm, and delightful.

41 WAGGONER, HYATT H. "Marianne Moore." In his American Poets:
    From the Puritans to the Present. Boston: Houghton Mifflin
    Co., pp. 364-68.
    Moore, not H. D., ought to be called the imagist. She
    followed Pound in his view of poetry as science, as anti-
    romantic. Her Selected Poems reads like the work of an
    editor who almost came to dislike poetry from reading too
    "much 'self-expressive,' pretentious, poorly controlled,
    vaguely romantic poetry." Her "Poetry" catalogues her likes
    and dislikes. She like the "genuine"--that is, things like
    hands, hair, and eyes. The function of the imagination for
    Moore is to shape the things or facts "into a sort of ordered
    structure." Eliot's praise of her poetry for being well
    written and using light rhyme is insufficient. And Moore's
    most "durable" poetry, "written after Eliot made his comment"
    (1935.8), goes beyond the limitations demanded by Moore's
    definition of the genuine.
    Excerpted: 1974.2.

42 WARLOW, FRANCIS W. "Moore's 'To a Snail.'" The Explicator,
    26 (February), item 51.

1969

"To a Snail" seems to lack Moore's characteristic use of particulars. But the snail serves as an analogue of the style discussed and demonstrated in the poem.

1969

1 ANON. "Preserving the Greensward." The New Yorker, 45 (8 March), 28-30.
Moore spoke briefly at a press conference held by the Save Central Park Committee. She said that Frederick Law Olmsted, one of the designers of Central Park, "wanted the people of the city to get the benefit of nature--a sense of enlarged freedom in limited space."

2 AUDEN, W. H. "A Mosaic for Marianne Moore." In his City without Walls and Other Poems. New York: Random House, pp. 24-25.
Reprint of 1967.10.

3 _____. "A Mosaic for Marianne Moore." Wilson Library Bulletin, 43 (March), 624-25.
Reprint of 1967.10.

4 BURKE, MICHAEL. "The Best Arm in Baseball." Wilson Library Bulletin, 43 (March), 622-23.
In 1967 we sent Moore a telegram asking her to throw out the first ball in our opening game in 1968. She showed up in midseason 1967 to practice. On opening day, she threw a "sinking slider" to catcher Frank Fernandez.

5 CLINES, FRANCIS X. "Elderly Protest at Parley Here." The New York Times, 3 May, p. 35.
Moore was named "Senior Citizen of the Year" at Governor Rockerfeller's Conference on the Aging.

6 CUMMINGS, E. E. Selected Letters of E. E. Cummings. Edited by F. W. Dupee and George Stade. New York: Harcourt, Brace & World, pp. 80, 110, 128, 162, 207, 208, 210, 273.
Three letters to Moore and various references to her.

7 DURSO, JOSEPH. "Marianne Moore, Baseball Fan." Saturday Review, 52 (12 July), 51-52,
Moore loves baseball because it is a game of precision.

8 EDSALL, CONSTANCE H. "Values and the Poems of Marianne Moore." English Journal, 58 (April), 516-18.

1969

The value of Moore's poetry resides in her "moral strength" and "artistic mastery." Her techniques allow her to write of conventional values without seeming a "tiresome moralist."

9 [FULLER, ROY B.] "Poets Today: Marianne Moore." In T. L. S.: Essays from the Times Literary Supplement, 1968. London: Oxford University Press, pp. 94-102.
Reprint of 1968.26.

10 GIFFORD, HENRY. "Two Philologists." In Marianne Moore: A Collection of Critical Essays (1969.28), pp. 172-78.
Moore and Emily Dickinson share certain feminine and American attributes, but their "essential kinship" resides in their revitalization of the English language, especially its Latin words, "by engaging [it] in the common labour of interpreting and assaying experience."
Excerpted: 1975.2 and 1976.1.

11 GOING, WILLIAM T. "Marianne Moore's 'Dream': Academic By-Path to Xanadu." In Studies in American Literature in Honor of Robert Dunn Faner, 1906-1967. A supplement to Papers on Language and Literature, 5 (Summer), 145-53.
Based on an exchange between Lionel Trilling and Jerome S. Shipman in Encounter, Moore's "Dream" is a bit of "elegant stichery." While the poem expresses partial agreement with Trilling and Shipman, it also is an ode to Bach, a fantasy that challenges one's sense of time, and a warning that genius cannot be subdued.

12 GRANT, DAMIAN. "Reviews and Comment." The Critical Quarterly, 11 (Summer), 191-92.
Moore's Complete Poems and Selected Poems (1969) reveal that she "domesticates" poetry. Her poems are made things --and sometimes more found than made.

13 HAMBURGER, MICHAEL. The Truth of Poetry: Tensions in Modern Poetry from Baudelaire to the 1960s. New York: Harcourt Brace Jovanovich, pp. 234-38, 252.
Moore's "Poetry" exemplifies the twentieth-century "tendency towards anti-poetry." It is an "anti-poem" because it could have been written in prose without much loss and because its argument takes precedence over music and emotion. Moreover, the form of the poem is mathematical rather than organic. Paradoxically, Moore's "obeisances to baseball fans and statisticians" and her "sacrifices of lyricism" are less likely to appeal to "the pragmatic majority" than the "utterly subjective lyricism of Dylan Thomas."

1969

14   JARRELL, RANDALL. "Fifty Years of American Poetry." In his
     The Third Book of Criticism. New York: Farrar, Straus &
     Giroux, pp. 315-19.
        Reprint of 1963.9.

15   JASKOWSKI, HELEN MARIE. "'A Method of Conclusions': A Criti-
     cal Study of the Poetry of Marianne Moore." Ph.D. disserta-
     tion, Stanford University, 248 pp. Abstracted in
     Dissertation Abstracts International, 30 (1969), 1137-38A.
        Moore has "a philosophy of particularism" that intuitively
     and emotionally apprehends objects as unique and both mate-
     rial and non-material. Her poems, themselves unique objects,
     record acts of perception. Looked at chronologically, Moore's
     poetry increasingly emphasizes intuitive, associative, non-
     rational perception and idiosyncratic form as it becomes
     narrower in subject matter and more sentimental.

16   MACKSEY, RICHARD A. "Marianne (Craig) Moore: A Brief Chro-
     nology." In Marianne Moore: A Collection of Critical
     Essays (1969.28), pp. 179-81.
        A list of major events in Moore's life to 1967.

17   MESSING, GORDON M. "The Linguistic Analysis of Some Contempo-
     rary Nonformal Poetry." Style, 2 (Fall), 327-28.
        The effects of Moore's "Critics and Connoisseurs" arise
     from features that are outside the scope of stylolinguistics.
     Although Moore makes use of rhyme and syllabic meter, her
     poems depend primarily on her "deftness in the choice and
     combination of words."

18   NITCHIE, GEORGE W. Marianne Moore: An Introduction to the
     Poetry. New York and London: Columbia University Press,
     x, 205 pp.
        Moore's poems typically contain both observation and
     exemplum, though the exempla are set in contexts that render
     them more exploratory than absolute. Throughout her work,
     "ethics and esthetics have a symbiotic relationship." Her
     eccentric prosody is a sort of opposition to prosody but
     also a safeguard against excess. Between Poems and Complete
     Poems, Moore has revised and abandoned many of her poems.
     Overall, the revisions seem more the product of whim (or
     sacrifice) than of system, and they make her poems seem more
     like continuing processes than like completed products. The
     arrangement of poems in Collected Poems and Complete Poems
     reflects Moore's "selective and changeable" sense of history.
     One group, violating the implied chronology, for example,
     consists of those poems that least successfully embody the

1969

tension of her two impulses--to generalize particulars and
to note them in their particularity. The chronology suggests that her worked moved from a "concern with life lived,
or failing to be lived, in terms of an esthetic of natural-
ness, fastidiousness, and enlightened self interest, to an
often humble examination of the partialities and objects of
concern that have no prior obligations to principles and
that are valued not because they illustrate a point but
because, illustrating only themselves they liberate emotion." The poems of the 1930s and '40s--some the result of
a personal crisis of confusion, of guilt and inadequacy, in
the face of World War II--are more affectionate and are more
explicit affirmations of human values. Her poems since Collected Poems tend toward self-parody and imply "some relaxing
of standards of self-criticism." Her art is a moral art,
with a reticence and rectitude that keep "at arm's length"
a knowledge of life as good and evil. Her poems are about
her mind, how "it moves from object to object." But unlike
Wordsworth, who saw his mind as a theater of the universe,
Moore sees "her own quirky consciousness."

19   PLIMPTON, GEORGE. "The World Series with Marianne Moore."
     Wilson Library Bulletin, 43 (March), 626-33.
          Reprint of 1964.25.

20   REGAN, ROBERT. Review of Nitchie's Marianne Moore (1969.18).
     Library Journal, 94 (1 October), 3451.
          Clear and sympathetic, Nitchie's study "should have a
     wide appeal."

21   RICKS, CHRISTOPHER. "Authority in Poems." The Southern Re-
     view, NS 5 (January), 208-209.
          Moore's Tell Me, Tell Me is "attenuated," causing one to
     wonder if she is "scraping the barrel." Moore is modest,
     but in print her self-depreciations seem "a begging bowl."
     Her rhyming is needless. She may be virtuous and ingenious--
     perhaps egocentric--but lacks "potency, diversity, or
     variety."

22   RIENHOLD, ROBERT. "Ousted Student Booed at Harvard for Grad-
     uation Talk." The New York Times, 13 June, p. 30.
          Moore received an honorary degree from Harvard today.

23   ROBINSON, EDGAR. "Four Lady Poets." Chicago Review, 21 (De-
     cember), 110-12.

1969

Moore's poetry has "the power of song"--but to little
purpose. It lacks passion and vision. But Moore is accurate, decent, sane, and courageous in her contemplation of
the world.

24 ROSENTHAL, M. L. "Comment." Poetry, 114 (May), 126-27.
Like Auden, Moore has broadened the scope of the lyric
by incorporating into it prose rhythms. For Complete Poems
she has revised "Poetry" and other poems and thus challenged
the notion of poems as closed systems.

25 SCHULMAN, GRACE. "Conversation with Marianne Moore." Quar-
terly Review of Literature, 16, nos, 1-2, 154-71.
An interview with Moore concerned primarily with Moore's
methods of composition but also with the publication of
Complete Poems, the oral reading of poetry, and the war in
Vietnam. Moore briefly discusses "To Victor Hugo of My Crow
Pluto," "I May, I Might, I Must," "Occasionem Cognosce,"
"Poetry," "O to Be a Dragon," "What Are Years," "Bach Plays
Bach" ("Dream"), "Marriage," "In Distrust of Merits," and
"The Paper Nautilus."

26 SPRAGUE, ROSEMARY. "Marianne Moore." In her Imaginary Gardens:
A Study of Five American Poets. Philadelphia: Chilton Book
Co., pp. 183-208.
Moore "is poetry itself." She writes with a knowledge
of literary tradition. She is most akin to certain eighteenth-century writers in her emphasis on poetry as instruc-
tive and fascinating and in her urbanity--though her form
rather resembles Gerard Manley Hopkins'. She also owes a
debt to Biblical and classical rhetoric. Mostly she is a
poet of the visual, the thing. (Includes biographical sketch.)

27 THÉRÈSE, SISTER. Marianne Moore: A Critical Essay. Contemporary Writers in Christian Perspective. [Grand Rapids,
Mich.]: William Eerdmans, 48 pp.
Moore has had a life of awards and acclaim. A poet of
the interaction of the visible and invisible, she presents
objects for themselves and then looks beyond them to their
"larger context" and implies "some wider meaning." Her
poems are "full of contrast and comparison"--of luxury and
simplicity and of animals and man, for example. Her syllabics differ from those of Robert Bridges and Dylan Thomas
in that she makes the stanza rather than the line the basic
unit. She uses rhythm, balance, parallelism, wit, irony,
juxtaposition, and quotation to create verbal structures
with external forms that release "inner experience." She

is a moralist, confronting man's mortality and his relationship to "something larger" than himself, and she expresses (often through the theme of silence) her ideal of the contemplative mind. Implicitly religious, her poetry is written from a Christian perspective and reflects a love of the world and a sense of its unity.
Excerpted: 1973.4.

28   TOMLINSON, CHARLES, ed. Marianne Moore: A Collection of Critical Essays. Twentieth Century Views. Englewood Cliffs, N.J.: Prentice-Hall, vi, 185 pp.
Tomlinson's "Introduction: Marianne Moore, Her Poetry and Her Critics" is an expansion of 1968.40. The collection contains an original essay by Gifford (1969.10), a chronology by Macksey (1969.16), a letter to Ezra Pound from Moore, and a selective bibliography of works about Moore. It reprints 1918.3, 1923.1, 1925.20, 1935.3, 1935.8, 1942.2, 1948.12, 1948.13, 1948.16, 1952.25, 1954.16, 1954.21, 1956.9, 1958.6, 1961.8, 1961.12, 1963.10, 1967.14.

29   UNTERECKER, JOHN. Voyager: A Life of Hart Crane. New York: Farrar, Straus and Giroux, pp. 173, 232, 294, 404, 405, 406, 407, 417, 480.
The story of Moore's editing of Crane's "Wine Menagerie" is "a jumble of badly managed gestures of good will." Crane listed Moore as a reference in his application to Otto Kahn for support. Crane regarded Moore and Harriet Monroe as a part of a tradition of effete and precious editors.

1970

1   ANON. Brief notice of Nitchie's Marianne Moore (1969.18). The Booklist, 66 (15 May), 1134.
The book is well written and appreciative.

2   ANON. "Museum Gets Work of Marianne Moore." The New York Times, 7 April, p. 41.
In an interview today, Clive Driver said that the Rosenbach Foundation has acquired Moore's literary and personal effects.

3   BACH, BERT C. Review of Tomlinson's Marianne Moore (1969.28). Library Journal, 95 (1 January), 69.
The collection is for academic libraries.

1970

4   BOGAN, LOUISE. <u>A Poet's Alphabet: Reflections on the Liter-ary Art and Vocation</u>. New York: McGraw-Hill Book Co., pp. 254-57. 303-306.
         Reprints 1944.4, 1954.4.

5   FRASER, G. S. "Quantitative Metres and Pure Syllabic Metres." In his <u>Metre, Rhyme, and Free Verse</u>. The Critical Idiom, 8. London: Methuen & Co., pp. 50, 52-54, 56.
         Syllabic verse has been more successful in America, where there is more "freedom and equality between syllabic units." The effect, in Moore's verse, for example, is "a very flat and dry, but also very painstaking, precision."

6   HALL, DONALD. <u>Marianne Moore: The Cage and the Animal</u>. Pegasus American Authors Series. New York: Pegasus, 199 pp.
         Caught by the surface brilliance of Moore's poetry, many critics have failed to hear "the dark music of feeling that informs" it. The clever technique of her early poems con-ceal "a young woman's vulnerable feelings." The poems in <u>Poems</u> and <u>Observations</u> reveal her preference for precision and clarity, a preference that is a matter of both taste and morality, yet contain some "astonishing images." The same preference and an adherence to standards are seen in her editorship of the <u>Dial</u>. The nine new poems of <u>Selected Poems</u> are less constrained, less acid, and more given to humor than the earlier poems, and they represent a turning inward. But in <u>The Pangolin and Other Verse</u> and <u>What Are Years</u>, the external world again becomes the focus--or the objectification of "the emotional threats, the metaphysical dangers that haunted Miss Moore's earlier poems." The style is less intricate and depends less on startling juxtaposi-tions. In her translation of La Fontaine, Moore shares his love of precision but adds a visual sense to his predomi-nantly intellectual verse. Some of the new poems in <u>Col-lected Poems</u> and <u>Like a Bulwark</u> have as a theme the strength achieved through humility and are less emotional and less direct in statement and syntax than those in <u>Nevertheless</u> and <u>What Are Years</u>. Much of Moore's late verse is light verse, occasioned by interest in some topic or object that is not, as in earlier poems, a starting place for an inward turning. But in <u>Tell Me, Tell Me</u> again objects are used "as a stimulus for meditation."
         Excerpted: 1975.2.

7   HAYES, ANN L. "On Reading Marianne Moore." In <u>A Modern Mis-cellany</u>. Carnegie Series in English, no. 11. Pittsburgh: Carnegie-Mellon University, pp. 1-19.

114

Neglected by critics, Moore is a poet of craft. "When I Buy Pictures" exemplifies the critical aesthetic of intensity and honesty that it argues. "The Student" shows her craft in syllabic measure and rhyme. "In Distrust of Merits," a fine war poem, is an "argument for self knowledge." "Sun," a religious poem, "shows Moore in full control" of craft, thought, and feeling. "Rescue with Yul Brynner" weaves "public event and private feeling." And "Dream" shows Moore's playfulness.

8   JENNINGS, ELIZABETH. "Marianne Moore." In <u>Contemporary Poets of the English Language</u>. Edited by Rosalie Murphy and James Vinson. Chicago and New York: St. James Press, pp. 767-70.
Moore's small subjects lead to grand themes. A "vivid shyness" prevents her from writing a personal poetry but does not make her a "cold writer." Her poetry is subtle in technique and moral in tone. She is "idiosyncratic" but not odd. (Includes brief biography and bibliography.)

9   JOOST, NICHOLAS and ALVIN SULLIVAN. <u>D. H. Lawrence and</u> The Dial. Carbondale: Southern Illinois University Press, pp. 25, 29-31, 34-35, 86, 94-113 ("Lawrence and <u>The Dial</u> of Marianne Moore"), 126, 128, 157, 167-78, 199-200, 202.
After Moore became editor in June 1925, Lawrence's work appeared in nineteen percent of the issues of the <u>Dial</u>. Moore admired his work. Hounded by censors, Lawrence sent the manuscript of <u>Pansies</u> through Moore to his agent. For the <u>Dial</u>, Moore selected eleven poems from the manuscript, which appears to have been an earlier version than that later published by Knopf. Moore's selection "reveals her own imagist bias as well as her taste and acuity as an editor."

10   KENNER, HUGH. "The Experience of the Eye: Marianne Moore's Tradition." In <u>Modern American Poetry: Essays in Criticism</u>. Edited by Jerome Mazzaro. New York: David McKay Co., pp. 204-21.
Reprint of 1965.14.

11   MARVIN, PATRICIA H. Review of Hall's <u>Marianne Moore</u> (1970.6). <u>Library Journal</u>, 95 (August), 2681.
Hall's book is "poetry criticism at its best" and is for all but the smallest libraries.

12   _____. Review of Sprague's <u>Imaginary Gardens</u> (1969.26). <u>Library Journal</u>, 95 (1 January), 69.
Sprague presents Moore with "penetration and admirable explication."

1970

13 PEARCE, ROY HARVEY. "The Critic as Advocate." The Southern
    Review, NS 6 (January), 237-40.
        Weatherhead's Edge of the Image (1967.29) is an essential
    introduction to Moore.

14 VONALT, LARRY P. "Marianne Moore's Medicines." The Sewanee
    Review, 78 (October-December), 669-78.
        Moore is a poet-physician, struggling against man's dis-
    eases of "affectation, arrogance, timidity, materialism,
    selfishness." Her medicines are "maxims" expressing "the
    idea that the spirit is stronger than the things of the
    world." Her observations of plants and animals reveal them
    to be guides to moral behavior. As in "The Steeple-Jack,"
    she attempts to integrate art and nature. The armor in her
    poetry is that of patience in adversity and thus that which
    can make man whole. Her poems are "antidotes" to self-
    righteousness. They are not "morbid."
        Excerpted: 1973.4.

15 WEINIG, SISTER MARY ANTHONY. Review of Hall's Marianne Moore
    (1970.6). Best Sellers, 30 (15 November), 349-50.
        Hall is more appreciative than incisive.

16 WILLIAMS, WILLIAM CARLOS. "Marianne Moore." In his Imagina-
    tions. Edited by Webster Schott. New York: New Directions,
    pp. 308-18.
        Reprint of 1925.20.

17 WILTSIE, NORMAN. "Imaginary Gardens." The New Leader, 53 (16
    March), 24.
        The appearance of Nitchie's study (1969.18) "demonstrates
    that Miss Moore's work is very much alive." Nitchie is
    fascinated by Moore's revisions, too intent on reducing her
    poetry to a Nitchie-an thought," and too fond of close anal-
    ysis to provide an introduction to Moore's poetry.

                              1971

1 CANE, MELVILLE. "Ladies of the Dial." The American Scholar,
   40 (Spring), 316-21.
       Moore criticized and revised my work when she was editor
   of the Dial. My experience with her demonstrated her cath-
   olic taste, seasoned judgment, and empathy with the poetic
   experience.

                              116

2   _____. "Ladies of the Dial." In his <u>Eloquent April</u>: <u>New</u>
       <u>Poems and Prose</u>. New York: Harcourt Brace Jovanovich, pp.
       48-65.
           Reprint of 1971.1.

3   ENGEL, BERNARD F. "Marianne Moore." <u>Contemporary Literature</u>,
       12 (Spring), 230-36.
           The publication of studies of Moore by Tomlinson
       (1969.28), Nitchie (1969.18), and Hall (1970.6) suggests
       that critics are beginning to penetrate the armor of Moore's
       poetry. Nitchie rightly sees in her work a tension between
       a concern for the nonhuman and human, her later work
       shifting to a stress on the latter concern. But Nitchies
       neglects the religious basis of the shift and the impor-
       tance of translating La Fontaine in working out the crisis
       the accompanied the shift. Hall's study is impressionistic,
       neo-Romantic--useful for its perceptive readings of indi-
       vidual poems.

4   FENDER, STEPHEN. Review of Nitchie's <u>Marianne Moore</u> (1969.18).
       <u>Journal of American Studies</u>, 5 (April), 110-12.
           Nitchie sometimes treats Moore preciously, as if she
       could not take care of herself. But he writes "close
       descriptive, analytical and evaluative criticism of the
       highest standard."

5   FULLER, ROY B. "An Artifice of Versification." In his <u>Owls</u>
       <u>and Artificers</u>: <u>Oxford Lectures on Poetry</u>. London: Andre
       Duetsch, pp. 44-68.
           An expansion of 1968.26, including an examination of
       Moore's syllabics in relationship to the theory and practice
       of Elizabeth Daryush.
           Excerpted: 1976.1.

6   GARRIGUE, JEAN. "Marianne Moore." In <u>Six American Poets from</u>
       <u>Emily Dickinson to the Present</u>: <u>An Introduction</u>. Edited
       by Allen Tate. Minneapolis: University of Minnesota Press,
       pp. 82-121, 239-41.
           Reprints 1965.10 with additions to include comments on
       <u>Complete Poems</u>, which is said to contain many revisions and
       exclusions and to add recent poems that are more "open,"
       less intricate.

7   JOOST, NICHOLAS and ALVIN SULLIVAN. <u>The Dial</u>: <u>Two Author</u>
       <u>Indexes</u>: <u>Anonymous & Pseudonymous Contributors</u>: <u>Contrib-</u>
       <u>utors in Clipsheets</u>. Bibliographic Contribution No. 6.
       Carbondale: The Libraries, Southern Illinois University,
       pp. 23-25, 46-47.

1971

> Identifies 124 unsigned "Briefer Mention" reviews and
> 42 editorial "Comments" as Moore's; lists her items that
> appeared in Dial clipsheets.
> See also 1975.11.

8   KENNER, HUGH. The Pound Era. Berkeley and Los Angeles: Uni-
     versity of California Press, pp. 16, 19, 68, 87-89, 166-68,
     319, 405, 507, 560.
         More than any other poem in English, Moore's "Bird-Witted"
     approximates Arnaut Daniel's rejection of conventional elo-
     quence. Its "technical felicities" must be seen from a
     distance that puts them in relationship to the structure of
     the whole poem and that is also required to see the meaning
     of the poem as "a parable of two forms of intelligence."

9   KINDLEY, JEFFREY BOWMAN. "Efforts of Affection: The Poetry
     of Marianne Moore." Ph.D. dissertation, Columbia University,
     189 pp. Abstracted in Dissertation Abstracts International,
     34 (1974), 7758-59A.
         Moore has been more acclaimed than understood. She uses
     a syllabic meter that is sometimes obscured through revi-
     sion and rearrangment. She has been influenced in technique
     and theme by such authors as James, Blake, Gordon Craig,
     Hardy, and minor prophets of the Bible. A number of her
     poems reveal her aesthetic principles, often misinterpreted
     ironies, musical rhythm, use of images of defense as meta-
     phors for spiritual integrity, and philosophy based on
     Christian doctrine.

10   McCORMICK, JOHN. The Middle Distance: A Comparative History
     of American Imaginative Literature, 1919-1932. New York:
     The Free Press, pp. ix, 123, 145, 153-56, 193, 194, 199.
         Moore is "a major-minor poet." She was not prolific, and
     one can trace little development in her work. In theme and
     technique, "In the Days of Prismatic Color" is typical of
     her idiosyncratic poetry. She writes with "elaborate
     brevity."

11   PEARCE, ROY HARVEY. Review of Nitchie's Marianne Moore
     (1969.18). American Literature, 42 (January), 602-603.
         Although Nitchie's explications overshadow his argument
     and although his book is not an introduction as its subtitle
     claims, it is the best study of Moore's poetry. It needs
     to be accompanied by a variorum edition of her work.

12   QUINN, SISTER M. BERNETTA. Review of Weatherhead's Edge of the
     Image (1967.29). Comparative Literature, 23 (Winter), 72-74.

Weatherhead is correct in ascribing to Moore and Williams a shared concern for clarity of image. Yet the world of Patterson is as alien to Moore as "her realm of precisely refined music" is to him.

13 _____. Review of Nitchie's Marianne Moore (1969.18). English Language Notes, 8 (March), 240-42.
Nitchie's "excellent study" stresses "the themes of adaptation and endurance characteristic of Miss Moore" and describes her "progress as a fight to be affectionate." His reading of "In Distrust of Merits" neglects Moore's Presbyterian faith. And his comparison of her with Stevens fails to show that she was concerned with things as they exist in ethical, not psychological or epistemological, relationships.

14 REPLOGLE, JUSTIN. "Marianne Moore and the Art of Intonation." Contemporary Literature, 12 (Winter), 1-17.
Moore controls the tunes, or "intonation contours," that readers make of her poetry. A "poetic talker" rather than singer, she uses punctuation and syntax to keep her poems incoherent until their parts are read with the proper intonation. Her method can be seen in "The Arctic Ox (or Goat)" and "For February 14th."

15 REXROTH, KENNETH. American Poetry in the Twentieth Century. New York: Herder and Herder, pp. 57, 68-70, 82.
Moore's poetry is "inhuman." Her poems are "tragic" in that they reveal armor grown "at the expense of the dweller within."
Excerpted: 1974.2 and 1976.1.

16 SCHULMAN, GRACE JAN. "Marianne Moore: The Poetry of Engagement." Ph.D. dissertation, New York University, 350 pp. Abstracted in Dissertation Abstracts International, 33 (1972), 765A.
In her poetry, Moore created a form with which to engage the important issues of the twentieth century. Central to the form are "techniques of argumentation," which tend to be "metaphysical" in her early work and dialectical in her later. The early work uses images to reveal argument; her later uses them to embody perceptual change. The basic rhythmic unit is not the line but the cadence of conversational phrases that reflect the movement of her argument.

1971

17   TAYLOR, CHRISTY M.   Review of Nitchie's <u>Marianne Moore</u>
     (1969.18).   <u>Studia neophilologica</u>, 43, no. 1, 325-26.
     Nitchie has written a good introduction to Moore.

18   WAND, DAVID HSIN-FU.   "The Dragon and the Kylin: The Use of
     Chinese Symbols and Myths in Marianne Moore's Poetry." <u>Lit-</u>
     <u>erature East and West</u>, 15, no. 3, 470-84.
     Moore's poetry abounds in references to Chinese art and
     myth. "Critics and Connoisseurs," "Bowls," "People's Sur-
     roundings," "He 'Digesteth Harde Yron,'" "Smooth Gnarled
     Crape Myrtle," and "Logic and the Magic Flute" refer to
     Chinese art objects. As she suggests in her reference to
     "rime prose" (or <u>fu</u>) in "In Lieu of the Lyre" and by her
     practice in "Blue Bug," she shares with classical Chinese
     poets the technique of using far-fetched associations. In
     "The Plumet Basilisk," "O to Be a Dragon," and "Nine Nec-
     tarines," she uses the Chinese dragon to represent the
     "qualities of flexibility and versatility."

1972

1   ANON.   "Brooklyn Rites for Marianne Moore." <u>The New York Times</u>,
     9 February, p. 42.
     Funeral services for Moore were held yesterday at the
     Lafayette Presbyterian Church, which she had attended for
     thirty-four years.

2   ANON.   "Marianne (Craig) Moore." <u>Current Biography</u>, 33 (March),
     46.
         Brief obituary.
         Reprinted: 1973.3.

3   ANON.   "Marianne Moore Dies." <u>The New York Times</u>, 6 February,
     pp. 1, 40.
     Moore died in her sleep yesterday at her home. She was
     eighty-four and for nearly two years had been a semi-invalid
     following a series of strokes. Her manuscripts and books
     will go to the Rosenbach Foundation. Its director, Clive
     Driver, will be her literary executor.

4   ANON.   "Marianne Moore Dies; Noted Poet." <u>Chicago Tribune</u>, 6
     February, sec. 4, p. 20.
     Associated Press obituary, which notes that Moore called
     her poems "things," that she kept three television sets
     going during baseball season, that she won various awards.

5   ANON. "Marianne Moore RIP." <u>National Review</u>, 24 (3 March), 207.
     Moore's poems present a world of "things firmly seized and possessed by the imagination." She had an ethos "involving discipline, restraint, concentration but also lightness, the striving for perfect form."

6   ANON. "Moore Will Lists Estate of $450,000." <u>The Washington Post</u>, 12 February, sec. B, p. 10.
     Moore left an estate of $450,000. Her brother, John Warner Moore, and her housekeeper, Gladys Elizabeth Berry, are mentioned in the will. Clive E. Driver is named as her literary executor.

7   ANON. "Nixon Mourns Death of Poet." <u>The Washington Post</u>, 7 February, Sec. C, p. 3.
     Nixon called Moore "one of our most distinguished poets."

8   ANON. "Obituary Notes." <u>Publishers Weekly</u>, 201 (7 February), 46.
     Moore died on 6 February at her home in Greenwich Village. (Includes a brief biography.)

9   ANON. "Transition." <u>Newsweek</u>, 79 (14 February), 86.
     The "high priestess" of American poetry died on 5 February. The Dodgers were her great love; she called her poems "things."

*10   CANNON, PATRICIA REARDON. "Marianne Moore: Poetics and the Quest for Poetry." Ph.D. dissertation, University of Chicago.
     Listed in <u>Comprehensive Dissertation Index, 1861-1972</u>, 30 (1973), 89.

11   ENGEL, BERNARD. "Marianne Moore, 1887-1972." <u>Society for the Study of Midwestern Literature Newsletter</u>, 2, no. 3, 6.
     Born a midwesterner, Moore is an American "poet of delight who is also a moralist." She set out to be a poet, not a female poet.

*12   GARELICK, JUDITH S. "Marianne Moore, Modern Poet: A Study of Miss Moore's Relationship with William Carlos Williams, E. E. Cummings, T. S. Eliot, Wallace Stevens, and Ezra Pound." Ph.D. dissertation, Harvard University, 244 pp.
     Listed in <u>Comprehensive Dissertation Index, 1981-1972</u>, 30 (1973), 89.

1972

13   GUILLORY, DANIEL LOUIS. "A Place for the Genuine: The Poetics
      of Marianne Moore." Ph.D. dissertation, Tulane University,
      161 pp. Abstracted in <u>Dissertation Abstracts International</u>,
      33 (1972), 1168A.
           Although she was at the center of developments that
      formed twentieth-century American poetry, Moore has been
      neglected by critics. Her modest aim in poetry was to use
      empirical observation to examine the things of the world
      and thus to free the imagination. The syllabic verse she
      developed was both unique and suited to her aim. Her poems
      fall into three groups: those concerned with aesthetic
      matters (e.g. "Poetry"); those that probe ethical questions,
      usually through observation of animals (e.g., "The Pango-
      lin"); and those that create an "Edenic landscape" (e.g.,
      "Virginia Britannia"). Her translations of La Fontaine's
      fables continued impulses present in her own work.

14   JANSON, DONALD. "Marianne Moore Room Set Up at Museum." <u>The</u>
      <u>New York Times</u>, 15 November, p. 36.
           Moore's Manhattan living room has been re-created at the
      Rosenbach Foundation Museum in Philadelphia.

15   LANE, GREY. <u>A Concordance to the Poems of Marianne Moore</u>.
      New York: Haskell House Publishers, x, 526 pp.
           A concordance keyed to <u>Complete Poems</u>. Divided into
      three parts: list of words and their occurrences, list of
      hyphenated compounds, list of word frequencies.

16   MORRIS, HARRY. "Poets and Critics, Critics and Poets." <u>The</u>
      <u>Sewanee Review</u>, 80 (October-December), 629-31.
           Though billed as a biography, Hall's <u>Marianne Moore</u>
      (1970.6) provides less biographical information than the
      <u>New York Times</u> obituary (1972.20). Hall seems not to have
      read much previous criticism of Moore. He informs us of
      his delights but does not "probe seriously" into Moore's
      work. More valuable are the brief passages in Bogan's <u>A</u>
      <u>Poet's Alphabet</u> (1970.4). Garrigue's pamphlet, the weakest
      of those gathered in <u>Six American Poets</u> (1971.6), is of
      more value than Hall's book or Bogan's passages.

17   SHERMAN, W. D. Review of Nitchie's <u>Marianne Moore</u> (1969.18).
      <u>Notes and Queries</u>, NS 19 (September), 356-57.
           Moore is more often acknowledged than read. Nitchie's
      book is of little help. It is condescending, quick to
      fabricate correspondences between Moore and other poets,
      and too concerned with expressing disappointment over the

exculsion of certain poems from Moore's various collections. In the poems of the last two decades, Moore sought to find and "preserve what she perceives as valuable in America."

18 STANFORD, DONALD E. "Marianne Moore (1887-1972)." The Southern Review, NS 8 (April), xi-xiii.
     Moore was "the last survivor" of the influential "experimentalist poets." Both times I had dealings with her (once in person, once by letter), I failed to understand her. Her poetry does not aim primarily at communication. It is witty and ironic, rarely involving "deeper feelings." In technique it is often brilliant. Its themes are moral ones.

19 WELL, MARTIN. "Marianne Moore, Famed U.S. Poet, Dies at 84." The Washington Post, 7 February, sec. C, p. 3.
     After suffering for two years from a heart ailment and a series of strokes, Moore died yesterday. During her career, she won many awards and wide acclaim. Her poetry incorporated bits of the world and transformed them.

20 WHITMAN, ALDEN. "Shaper of Subtle Images." The New York Times, 6 February, p. 40.
     Long obituary. Moore "was one of the country's most laureled poets and among its most ingenuous talkers and public personalities. Includes biographical sketch and quotations from Sargeant's New Yorker profile (1957.27).

1973

1 ABBOTT, CRAIG S. "Marianne Moore: A Descriptive Bibliography." Ph.D. dissertation, University of Texas at Austin. 392 pp. Abstracted in Dissertation Abstracts International, 34 (1974), 5951-52A. A revised, altered in format, and expanded version published in 1977 by the University of Pittsburgh Press in its Pittsburgh Series in Bibliography.
     Lists or describes Moore's works to appear during her lifetime—including separately published works, contributions of prose and poetry to books and periodicals, translations by and of Moore, drawings, recordings, letters, editorial work. Records the textual variants in reprintings of her books.

2 ANON. "Briefs on the Arts. Tree Fund Honors Poet." The New York Times, 16 January, p. 35.

1973

> The Greensward Foundation has created a memorial fund
> for Moore, who was president of the foundation from 1964
> until her death on 5 February 1972. Her poem "Camperdown
> Elm" celebrated "our crowning curio" and helped save the
> tree.

3   ANON. "Marianne (Craig) Moore." In Current Biography Yearbook,
     1972. Edited by Charles Moritz. New York: The H. W.
     Wilson Co., p. 467.
         Reprint of 1972.2.

4   ANON. "Marianne Moore." In Contemporary Literary Criticism.
     Vol. 1. Edited by Carolyn Riley. Detroit: Gale, pp.
     226-30.
         Excerpts from 1953.13, 1960.18, 1962.8, 1964.9, 1965.10,
     1969.27, 1970.14.

5   ANON. "Notes on People." The New York Times, 3 November, p.
     17.
         Wallace Stegner and Gwendolyn Brooks will replace Conrad
     Aiken and Moore, both dead, as honorary consultants in Amer-
     ican letters to the Library of Congress.

6   ANON. "Philadelphia Loan." The New Yorker, 44 (9 June), 26.
         In an address to the Grolier Club on the occasion of its
     exhibition of material from the Rosenbach Foundation, Clive
     E. Driver explained that the Foundation recently purchased
     Moore's literary effects. After the address, Driver told
     how he had visited Moore and obtained the material.

7   BOGAN, LOUISE. What the Woman Lived: Selected Letters of
     Louise Bogan, 1920-1970. Edited by Ruth Limmer. New York:
     Harcourt Brace Jovanovich, pp. 223, 235-36, 242-43, 245,
     260, 261, 276, 278, 287-88, 308, 336, 338, 352, 381.
         Includes passing references to Moore--Bogan's reactions
     to her books, to Moore's appearance at various gatherings,
     to Moore's attending a YMHA class, and so forth. Also in-
     cludes discussion of Bogan's votes for Moore to receive the
     Harriet Monroe poetry award and the Bollingen Prize.

8   GLATSTEIN, JACOB. "The Poetry of Marianne Moore." Translated
     from Yiddish by Doris Vidaver. Prairie Schooner, 47 (Sum-
     mer), 133-41.
         Translation of 1947.4.

9   GREENHOUSE, LINDA. "Literary Tour of the 'Village' Offers a
     Glimpse of Its Golden Age." The New York Times, 20 July,
     p. 33.

Moore's residence from 1918 to 1929 (14 St. Luke's Place) was one home visited by 300 people who took part in a two-hour Village Literary Walk.

10   HADAS, PAMELA GAY. "Efforts of Affection: The Poetry of Marianne Moore." Ph.D. dissertation, Washington University, 273 pp. Abstracted in <u>Dissertation Abstracts International</u>, 34 (1973), 2561A. Published in 1977 as <u>Marianne Moore: Poet of Affection</u> by Syracuse University Press.
   Central to the style and substance of Moore's poetry is the paradox of wanting to be at once explicit and restrained. Her poems are, in her phrase, "efforts of affection"--attempts to connect objects, ideas, and people with the self. They are both objective and revelatory of personal motives.

11   JACOBSON, JOSEPHINE. "From Ann to Marianne: Some Women in American Poetry." In <u>Two Lectures</u>. Washington, D. C.: Library of Congress, pp. 19, 21.
   Moore and Dickinson were alike in a number of ways. Both drew their poems from other than the "events and circumstantial changes in their own lives." Moore raises observation to love.

12   POUND, EZRA. "Marianne Moore and Mina Loy." In his <u>Selected Prose, 1909-1965</u>. Edited by William Cookson. New York: New Directions, pp. 424-25.
   Reprint of 1918.3.

13   SEGNITZ, BARBARA, and CAROL RAINEY. "Introduction." In their <u>Psyche: The Feminine Poetic Consciousness: An Anthology of Modern American Women Poets</u>. New York: The Dial Press, pp. 28-31.
   Moore is among a group of poets (including May Swenson and Elizabeth Bishop) who choose "neither to play the traditional woman's role nor to react against it" and thus who are "victimized," honoring the "traditional definition with their respectability and civilized attitudes." Moore's subject is the mind's apprehension of things.

14   STALLKNECHT, NEWTON P. "Poetry and the Lure of the Real: Some Reflections on S. T. Coleridge, Wallace Stevens and Marianne Moore." In <u>Texte und Kontext: Studien zur deutschen und vergleichenden literaturwissenschaft: Festschrift fur Norbert Fuerst zum 65. Geburtstag</u>. Edited by Manfred Durzak, Eberhard Reichmann, and Ulrich Weisstein. Bern: Francke, pp. 271-74.

1973

> Many of Moore's poems seem "a fascinated surrender of
> attention to the features of an attractive object." Her
> poems, like Stevens', seek not to make statements but to
> provide an "encounter" with something.

15   SUTTON, WALTER. "Marianne Moore." In his <u>American Free Verse:
     The Modern Revolution in Poetry</u>. New York: New Directions,
     pp. 103-17.
>   Unlike other free-verse poets, Moore observes "a strict
>   measure or count of syllables." Syllabic verse combines
>   freedom and discipline. Moore's aesthetic of organic form
>   is contained in her imagistic poem "To a Snail." "He 'Di-
>   gesteth Harde Yron,'" "The Pangolin," "The Paper Nautilus,"
>   "The Wood-Weasel," "A Grave," "What Are Years," "The
>   Steeple-Jack," "The Fish," "To a Steam Roller," and other
>   poems reveal the suitability of her metric and method to
>   her intelligence.

16   UNTERMEYER, LOUIS. "Marianne Moore." In his <u>50 Modern Amer-
     ican & British Poets, 1920-1970</u>. New York: David McKay
     Co., pp. 243-46.
>   Moore's verse is constructed of quotations and "keen
>   descriptions," based on a syllabic meter, and made tense by
>   the interplay of rhyme and accent. Moore sought precision
>   and clarity. "Nevertheless" and "The Mind Is an Enchanting
>   Thing" are typical.

17   WINTERS, YVOR. "Holiday and Day of Wrath." In his <u>Uncollected
     Essays and Reviews</u>. Edited by Francis Murphy. Chicago:
     The Swallow Press, pp. 22-26.
>   Reprint of 1925.22.

1974

1   ABBOTT, CRAIG S. Review of Lane's <u>Concordance to the Poems of
    Marianne Moore</u> (1972.15). <u>Computers and the Humanities</u>, 8
    (January), 56-57.
>   The concordance makes some alterations of Moore's text
>   but does not take into account an errata slip issued with
>   <u>Complete Poems</u> and printed in the British impression of the
>   book.

2   ANON. "Marianne Moore." In <u>Contemporary Literary Criticism</u>.
    Vol. 2. Edited by Carolyn Riley and Barbara Harte. De-
    troit: Gale Research Co, pp. 290-92.
>   Excerpts from 1952.19, 1963.9, 1965.8, 1966.14, 1968.21,
>   1968.29, 1968.41, 1971.15.

3   GARRIGUE, JEAN. "Marianne Moore." In <u>American Writers: A</u>
     <u>Collection of Literary Biographies</u>. Edited by Leonard
     Unger. Vol. 3. New York: Charles Scribner's Sons, pp.
     193-217.
          Reprint of 1965.10.

4   GUILLORY, DANIEL L. "Hart Crane, Marianne Moore, and the
     Brooklyn Bridge." <u>Ball State University Forum</u>, 15 (Sum-
     mer), 48-49.
          Crane's "Proem: To Brooklyn Bridge" is a major source
     of inspiration for Moore's "Granite and Steel." Moore ex-
     pands lines from Crane and shares his view of "the libera-
     ting effect that the bridge has on its beholder." Yet her
     approach differs from his: Crane saw the bridge as "an
     agent of transcendence"; Moore saw it as a tangible monu-
     ment to the heroic discipline that created it.

5   O'SULLIVAN, MAURICE J., Jr. "Native Genius for Disunion:
     Marianne Moore's 'Spenser's Ireland.'" <u>Concerning Poetry</u>,
     7 (Fall), 42-47.
          In "Spenser's Ireland" Moore defines the Irish nature
     and turns the definition on herself, thus seeing her "Irish
     relentlessness," "her inability to submit in silence," and
     her dissatisfaction that arises from "the lack of union
     between desire and reality."

6   STAUFFER, DONALD BARLOW. <u>A Short History of American Poetry</u>.
     New York: E. P. Dutton & Co., pp. 275, 292, 297-302, 343,
     366.
          Moore devoted her attention to technique, writing poems
     that are "constructions" designed for eye as well as ear.
     Her syllabic stanzas owe much to the haiku. Her rhymes are
     subtle and ingenious. Her poems are precise in language
     and thought, though ideas are subordinated to "the play of
     intelligence" among images, objects, and quotations.
     Elizabeth Bishop has been influenced by her.

                              1975

1   ABBOTT, CRAIG S. "A System of Bibliographical Reference Num-
     bering. <u>Papers of the Bibliographical Society of America</u>,
     69 (January-March), 73-74.
          Moore's "Poetry" provides an example for a system of
     numbering that can be used in indexes of textual variants.

1975

2   ANON. "Marianne Moore." In <u>Contemporary Literary Criticism</u>.
Vol. 4. Edited by Carolyn Riley. Detroit: Gale Research
Co., pp. 358-65.
Excerpts from 1954.21, 1958.6, 1958.10, 1965.14, 1967.29,
1969.10, 1969.26, 1970.6, 1972.18, 1973.8, 1973.15.

3   BAR-YAACOV, LOIS. "Marianne Moore: An 'In-Patriot.'" <u>The</u>
<u>Hebrew University Studies in Literature</u>, 3 (Autumn), 165-95.
Moore's work coincides at many points with the theories
of Pound. But critics have failed to see its more important
affinities with Emerson and Thoreau and with the Puritans.
Like them, she disliked "the purely decorative," liked the
functional and factual, rejected "convention in favor of
self-reliance," celebrated "life's mysteries and inconsis-
tencies," rejected "aspirations toward closed philosophical
systems and artistic perfection," denied a conflict between
science and religion, and was preoccupied with moral choice.
These affinities can be seen in "England," "New York,"
"Poetry," "An Octopus," "To Statecraft Embalmed," "The
Jerboa," "He 'Digesteth Harde Yron,'" "The Pangolin," and
"In the Days of Prismatic Color."

4   CULLER, JONATHAN. <u>Structuralist Poetics: Structuralism,</u>
<u>Linguistics, and the Study of Literature</u>. Ithaca: Cornell
University Press, pp. 150-51.
Like many other poems that refer to the artificiality of
poetry, Moore's "Poetry" does not attempt to go beyond the
artificiality but merely forestalls objections to it.

5   ENGEL, BERNARD F. "Moore's 'A Face.'" <u>The Explicator</u>, 34
(December), item 29.
Moore's "A Face" can be read as another of her celebra-
tions of the "values of 'order, ardour, uncircuitous simplicity'" rather than as a casually offered and passing
notion or as the product of an emotional or philosophical
crisis.

6   KENNER, HUGH. "Disliking It." In his <u>A Homemade World: The</u>
<u>American Modernist Writers</u>. New York: Alfred A Knopf, pp.
91-118.
A revision of 1965.14, which has been expanded to include
a discussion of Moore's influence on Williams (especially
in the view of a poem as language exhibited rather than
uttered) and to include discussion prompted by <u>Complete</u>
<u>Poems</u>.

7   KUNITZ, STANLEY. <u>A Kind of Order, A Kind of Folly: Essays
    and Conversations</u>. Boston: Little, Brown and Co., pp.
    220-27.
        Reprint of 1941,10, 1964.20.

8   MOORE, GEOFFREY. "American Poetry and the English Language."
    In <u>American Literature since 1900</u>. Edited by Marcus
    Cunliffe. London: Barrie & Jenkins Ltd., pp. 104, 109,
    124, 128-32, 139.
        Moore was "an experimenter in her strange collocation of
    facts and abstruse references...and in her syllabic-counting."
    Her syllabic verse "has a validity of its own" and a lineage
    in Welsh verse.

9   RAINEY, CAROL. "The Poetic Theory of Marianne Moore." Ph.D.
    dissertation, University of Cincinnati, 157 pp. Abstracted
    in <u>Dissertation Abstracts International</u>, 36 (1976), 6103A.
        Moore's theory of poetry combines the romantic doctrine
    that the poem is shaped by the personality of the poet and
    the classical emphasis on control and restraint. Moore
    views poems as objectifications, through factual description,
    of the artist's feelings. Precision of observation of the
    objective world implies the validity of the poet's convic-
    tion that led to the observation.

10 STELOFF, FRANCIS. "Marianne Moore." In her <u>In Touch with
    Genius,</u> which is printed in full in <u>Journal of Modern Lit-
    erature,</u> 4 (April), 870-77. Special Gotham Book Mart Issue.
        Recalls Moore's association with her and the Gotham Book
    Mart.

11 ZINGMAN, BARBARA. The Dial: <u>An Author Index.</u> Troy, N.Y.:
    Whitson Publishing Co., pp. v-xxi, 149-59.
        Moore became acting editor of the <u>Dial</u> in June 1925.
    Her editorial comments were not as "far-ranging in subject
    matter" as Scofield Thayer's. The index lists twelve of
    Moore's poems, seventeen of her signed book reviews, 102 of
    her anonymous "Briefer Mention" reviews, and four of her
    editorial "Comments."
        <u>See also</u> 1971.7.

1976

1 ANON. "Marianne Moore." In <u>Modern American Literature</u>. Edited by Dorothy Nyren, Maurice Kramer, and Elaine Fialka
   Kramer. Vol. 4 of <u>A Library of Literary Criticism</u>. New
   York: Frederick Ungar Publishing Co., pp. 316-18.
       Excerpts of 1968.21, 1969.10, 1969.18, 1969.28, 1971.5,
   1971.15.

2 AUDEN, W. H. "A Mosaic for Marianne Moore." In his <u>Collected</u>
   <u>Poems</u>. Edited by Edward Mendelson. New York: Random House,
   p. 577.
       Reprint of 1967.10.

3 EDMISTON, SUSAN, and LINDA D. CIRINO. <u>Literary New York: A</u>
   <u>History and Guide</u>. Boston: Houghton Mifflin Co., pp. 62,
   70-71, 79-81, 89, 100, 105, 108, 156, 216, 334, 335, 345,
   355-56, 361-63.
       In 1918 Moore moved from New Jersey to an apartment at
   14 St. Luke's Place in Greenwich Village. She was among
   those who gathered on Sundays at Alfred Kreymborg's home
   in Grantwood, New Jersey, and then, in 1915, at his apartment on Bank Street in the Village. During the years of
   the <u>Dial</u>, she often met with others at Paul Rosenfeld's
   apartment on Irving Place. She moved to 260 Cumberland
   Avenue in Brooklyn in 1929 and later to 35 West 9th Street
   in Manhattan.

4 HEYMAN, C. DAVID. <u>Ezra Pound: The Last Rower</u>. New York:
   Viking Press, A Richard Seaver Book, pp. 34, 49, 61, 87,
   94, 214-15, 250, 277, 294, 299, 313.
       While in St. Elizabeth's Hospital, Pound helped Moore
   with her translation of La Fontaine. Several months before
   his death he read her "What Are Years" at a memorial service
   for her.

5 OLSON, ELDER. "The Poetry of Marianne Moore." In his <u>On Value</u>
   <u>Judgments in the Arts and Other Essays</u>. Chicago: The University of Chicago Press, pp. 50-54.
       Reprint of 1957.23.

6 RANTA, JERRALD. "Palindromes, Poems, and Geometric Form."
   <u>Visible Language</u>, 10 (Spring), 164-67.
       Moore's "To a Chameleon" is palindromic in rhyme, shape,
   and line arrangement.

1976

7   WILLIS, PATRICIA C. and CLIVE E. DRIVER. "Bibliographical
        Numbering and Marianne Moore." Papers of the Bibliograph-
        ical Society of America, 70 (April-June), 261-63.
            Abbott's system of numbering (1975.1) does not and cannot
        reflect the complexity of the full history of Moore's
        "Poetry."

Index

This is primarily an index to names and titles. It includes the names of authors of works about Moore and the names of people mentioned in the abstracts. It includes the titles of articles, parts of books, and books about Moore and the titles of Moore's works mentioned in the abstracts. (Readers seeking discussions of individual works by Moore should be aware that, especially in abstracts of lengthy articles and books, I have not mentioned every work by Moore that is discussed.) The index also includes these subject entries: bibliography, biography, criticism (collections of and surveys of), dissertations, interviews, manuscripts, and obituaries.

H. S. <u>See</u> Smith, Harrison
Hadas, Pamela Gay, 1973.10
"Half Deity," 1942.2
Hall, Donald, 1961.8-9; 1963.8;
    1965.11; 1970.6, 11, 15;
    1971.3; 1972.16
Hamburger, Michael, 1969.13
Hammel, Liza, 1965.12
Hardy, Thomas, 1971.9
<u>Hart Crane: A Biographical and
    Critical Study</u>, 1948.15
"Hart Crane, Marianne Moore, and
    the Brooklyn Bridge," 1974.4
<u>Hart Crane: The Life of an Amer-
    ican Poet</u>, 1937.2
Hartley, Marsden, 1945.7
Hartsock, Mildred, 1962.12
Hawkins, A. Desmond, 1935.10
Hayakawa, S. I., 1945.8
Hayes, Ann L., 1970.7
Hazel, Robert, 1964.13
"Heart of the Thing, The,"
    1956.22
Hecht, Anthony, 1959.6; 1968.29
"He 'Digesteth Harde Yron,'"
    1948.12-13; 1954.24; 1966.6;
    1967.29; 1971.18; 1973.15;
    1975.3
Heiney, Donald, 1958.9
"He Made This Screen," 1923.5
Hemingway, Ernest, 1965.14
Herbert, George, 1962.16
"Hero, The," 1935.3; 1954.24;
    1960.4; 1966.6
Hersey, John, 1964.14
"Her Shield," 1953.12
Heyman, C. David, 1976.4
"His Shield," 1954.24; 1960.18;
    1963.4
<u>History of American Poetry, 1900-
    1940, A</u>, 1946.7
Hochman, Sandra, 1967.20
Hoffman, Daniel G., 1952.22;
    1953.10; 1960.10; 1967.22
Hoffman, Frederick J., 1946.8;
    1953.11; 1955.17
"Holiday and Day of Wrath,"
    1925.22; 1973.17
Holmes, John, 1957.16
<u>Homemade World, A</u>, 1975.6

"Hometown Piece for Messrs.
    Alston and Reese," 1956.4;
    1959.6; 1960.9, 16, 19
Honig, Edwin, 1952.23; 1955.18
Hopkins, Gerard Manley, 1937.3;
    1952.27; 1969.26
Horder, John, 1964.15
Horton, Philip, 1937.2
Hough, Graham, 1957.17
Howard, Jane, 1967.22
Howe, Irving, 1955.19
Howes, Barbara, 1966.13
Hoyt, Helen, 1918.2
Hughes, Langston, 1952.6;
    1967.19
Hugo, Victor, 1964.21
"Humble Animal, The," 1942.4;
    1951.9; 1953.13
"Humility, Concentration, and
    Gusto," 1956.9
Humphries, Rolfe, 1925.7; 1954.24
Hutchens, John K., 1954.12
Hyman, Stanley Edgar, 1961.10;
    1966.14

"Icosasphere, The," 1958.8
"Ideas of the Meaning of Form,"
    1961.7
<u>Idiosyncrasy & Technique</u>, 1958.15
"If Not Silence, Then Restraint,"
    1957.16
Ignatow, David, 1964.33
"Illustration," 1968.3
"Imagery of Marianne Moore, The,"
    1956.16
"Imaginary Garden, The," 1948.7
"Imaginary Gardens," 1970.17
<u>Imaginary Gardens</u>, 1969.26
"Imagination and Fancy: Robert
    Lowell and Marianne Moore,"
    1964.39
<u>Imaginations</u>, 1970.16
<u>Imagism: A Chapter for the
    History of Modern Poetry</u>,
    1951.8
"I May, I Might, I Must," 1969.25
"In a Collector's Pleasure Is
    Pleasure to Share," 1961.6
In Defense of Reason, 1947.6

Knoll, Robert E., 1962.18
Koch, Kenneth, 1957.18
Koch, Vivienne, 1948.8; 1950.1
Kreymborg, Alfred. 1918.1:
    1920.1; 1921.3; 1925.8;
    1929.2; 1946.8; 1953.11;
    1957.5: 1963.21: 1976.3
Kunitz, Stanley J., 1941.10;
    1942.1; 1955.3; 1960.13;
    1964.20; 1966.16; 1975.7

"Labors of Hercules," 1964.23
"Ladies' Day," 1944.8
"Ladies' Day on Parnassus,"
    1957.26
"Ladies of the Dial," 1971.1-2
La Fontaine, Jean de, 1948.8;
    1953.9; 1956.20; 1957.18;
    1960.15, 18; 1967.9. See
    also Fables of La Fontaine,
    The
Laforgue, Jules, 1918.2, 3;
    1929.5
Lane, Gary, 1972.15; 1974.1
Langland, John, 1954.18
Language as Gesture, 1952.15
La poésie américaine moderniste,
    1910-1940, 1948.11
Larsson, R. Ellsworth, 1926.9
Lask, Thomas, 1963.11; 1966.15-16
"Lasting Contribution of Ezra
    Pound, The," 1965.9
Lattimore, Richmond, 1955.22
Laughlin, J., 1964.33
Lawrence, D. H., 1970.8
"Leading Lady of U.S. Verse,"
    1967.22
"Lead-Off Lady," 1968.4
Leavis, F. R., 1935.13
Le Breton, Maurice, 1947.5
Lechlitner, Ruth, 1935.14;
    1941.11
Lecture de la poésie américaine,
    1968.23
Legler, Philip F., 1953.14
"Leonardo da Vinci's," 1959.11;
    1967.29
"Les avatars de l'imagisme,"
    1968.23
"Letter for Your Birthday, A,"
    1964.31

"Letter from Kathleen Raine, A,"
    1964.26
Letters of Ezra Pound, The,
    1950.2
Letters of Wallace Stevens,
    1966.23
Levin, Harry, 1954.14; 1964.21
Lewis, Anthony, 1958.11
Lewis, H. D., 1948.13
Lewis, May, 1936.4
Lewis, R. W. B., 1967.25
Libby, Margaret Sherwood,
    1963.12
"Liberator of Poems, A," 1952.17
"Library Lists Verse of Marianne
    Moore," 1958.3
Library of Literary Criticism,
    1960.17; 1976.1
Life among the Surrealists,
    1962.15
"Life Goes on a Zoo Tour with a
    Famous Poet," 1953.3
"Light Is Speech," 1958.7
"Like a Bulwark," 1923.5
Like a Bulwark, 1956.3, 12, 14-15,
    22; 1957.2-3, 7, 9-11, 13-15,
    17-19, 21, 23, 26, 28, 30-32;
    1963.4; 1970.6
"Likings of an Observationist,"
    1956.9
Lindquist, Jennie D., 1946.9
L'Influence du symbolisme français
    sur la poésie Américaine,
    1929.5
"Linguistic Analysis of Some Con-
    temporary Nonformal Poetry,"
    1969.17
"Listener's Book Chronicle, The,"
    1957.3
"Literalist of the Imagination,
    A," 1925.11-12; 1936.5;
    1937.4
Literary History of the United
    States, 1948.9
Literary New York, 1976.3
Literary Opinion in America,
    1937.4
"Literary Tour of the Village,"
    1973.9
"Literature in Verse?" 1951.7

Little Magazine: A History and
  Bibliography, The, 1946.8
Little Review Anthology, The,
  1953.1, 16
Lives of the Poets, 1959.12
"Logic and the Magic Flute,"
  1971.18
Lohf, Kenneth A., 1958.16–17
"Lords of a New Language,"
  1962.10
Lowell, Amy, 1923.2
Lowell, Robert, 1962.4; 1964.22,
  25, 39; 1967.19, 29
Loy, Mina, 1918.3; 1953.16;
  1973.12
Lundy, Gerald, 1965.15
Lyly, John, 1925.3; 1941.2

M. D. Z. See Zabel, Morton
  Dauwen
M. F. C., 1956.13
M. G. D., 1945.10
M. J. See Josephson, Matthew
McAlmon, Robert, 1931.1; 1962.18
McAlmon and the Lost Generation,
  1962.18
McBride, Henry, 1959.7
McCord, Howard, 1964.23
McCormick, John, 1971.10
"M'Cracken Attacks Ad Agencies'
  Role," 1958.4
McDonald, Gerald D., 1952.26;
  1954.19; 1955.23; 1957.19
"MacDowell Colony, 50 Years Old,
  Hails Marianne Moore,"
  1967.4
Macksey, Richard A., 1969.16
MacLeish, Archibald, 1963.21
Maddocks, Melvin, 1956.14;
  1966.17; 1967.26
Magic Maker: E. E. Cummings,
  The, 1958.13
"Maiden, The," 1960.8
"Major Poet, Minor Verse,"
  1959.2
"Make It New: Poetry, 1920–
  1950," 1960.20
Mallarmé, Stéphane, 1929.5
Mann, Thomas, 1963.21
Manuscripts, 1963.19; 1970.2;
  1972.3, 6, 14; 1973.6

"Marianne (Craig) Moore,"
  1952.9; 1953.4; 1968.5;
  1972.2; 1973.3
"Marianne (Craig) Moore: A Brief
  Chronology," 1969.16
"Marianne Moore," 1916.1; 1920.2;
  1923.1; 1925.10, 18, 20;
  1929.5; 1932.2; 1935.13, 21;
  1947.5; 1948.11, 16; 1952.21;
  1954.25–26; 1957.33; 1958.9;
  1960.17; 1961.12; 1962.16;
  1963.19; 1965.7; 1966.24;
  1967.11; 1968.18, 19, 41;
  1969.26; 1970.8, 16; 1971.3;
  1973.4, 15, 16; 1974.2–3;
  1975.2, 10; 1976.1
Marianne Moore (Engel), 1964.9
Marianne Moore (Garrigue),
  1965.10; 1971.6; 1974.3
"Marianne Moore, 1887–1972"
  (Engel), 1972.11
"Marianne Moore (1887–1972)"
  (Stanford), 1972.18
Marianne Moore: A Collection of
  Critical Essays, 1969.28
Marianne Moore: A Critical Essay,
  1969.27
"Marianne Moore: A Descriptive
  Bibliography," 1973.1
"Marianne Moore: An Apprecia-
  tion," 1936.4
"Marianne Moore: An 'In Patri-
  ot,'" 1975.3
Marianne Moore: An Introduction
  to the Poetry, 1969.18
"Marianne Moore: A 'Salvo of
  Barks,'" 1962.12
"Marianne Moore: Autumn 1966,"
  1968.34
"Marianne Moore, Baseball Fan,"
  1969.7
"Marianne Moore, 81 Today, Given
  Literature Medal," 1968.27
"Marianne Moore: Her Poetry and
  Her Critics," 1968.40
"Marianne Moore: Imaginary Gar-
  dens and Real Toads," 1953.11
"Marianne Moore, Modern Poet,"
  1972.12

"Method of Conclusions: A Critical Study of the Poetry of Marianne Moore," 1969.15
"Method of Marianne Moore, The," 1935.3; 1952.15; 1957.6
Metre, Rhyme, and Free Verse, 1970.5
"Middle Age and Two Possible Wives," 1954.22
Middle Distance, The, 1971.10
Miles, Josephine, 1966.18
Millay, Edna St. Vincent, 1921.3; 1925.12
Miller, Lois, 1963.14
Miller, Mary Owings, 1943.1; 1955.24
Millet, Fred B., 1940.3
"Mind and Matter," 1945.8
"Mind Is an Enchanting Thing, The," 1945.6; 1957.25; 1966.6 1973.16
"Miracle of Integrity and Wit," 1952.27
"Miss Marianne Moore," 1925.2
"Miss Marianne Moore's Zoo," 1948.4
"Miss Moore," 1953.10; 1957.22; 1968.24
"Miss Moore Herself," 1966.13
"Miss Moore in Manhattan," 1966.2
"Miss Moore Is Herself," 1955.24
"Miss Moore Keeps to Narrow Path," 1952.20
"Miss Moore's Art Is Not a Democratic One," 1925.6
"Miss Moore's Observations," 1923.5
Mizener, Arthur, 1954.20
Modern American Poetry, 1925.18
Modern Miscellany, A, 1970.7
Modern Poet: Essays from The Review, The, 1968.19
Modern Poetry: Essays in Criticism, 1968.15
"Modern Poetry: The American Accent," 1957.13
Modern Poets: A Critical Introduction, The, 1960.18
Moliere, 1964.21
"Monkey Puzzle, The," 1935.3

"Monkeys, The," 1963.14; 1964.12. See also "My Apish Counsins"
Monro, Harold, 1964.1
Monroe, Harriet, 1920.1; 1922.3; 1938.1; 1950.2; 1969.29
Montaigne, Michel Eyquem de, 1964.21
Moore, Geoffrey, 1975.8
Moore, George, 1925.12
Moore, John Warner, 1972.6
Moore, Nicholas, 1964.33
"Moore: 'Spenser's Ireland,'" 1966.18
"Moore's 'A Face,'" 1975.5
"Moore's 'In Distrust of Merits,'" 1952.2
"Moore's 'See in the Midst of Fair Leaves,'" 1952.22
"Moore's 'The Fish,'" 1949.3; 1962.22
"Moore's 'The Icosasphere,'" 1958.8
"Moore's 'To a Snail,'" 1968.42
"Moore Will Lists Estate of $450,000," 1972.6
"Moorish Georgeousness," 1967.14
"More about Moore," 1947.1
More Modern American Poets, 1954.25
Morris, Harry, 1972.16
Morse, Samuel French, 1957.20; 1960.14; 1968.32
"Mosaic for Marianne Moore, A," 1967.10; 1969.2, 3
Moss, Howard, 1964.33
"Motives and Motifs in the Poetry of Marianne Moore," 1942.2; 1945.5; 1946.4; 1968.15
"Much Honored Poet Wins National Institute Prize," 1953.5
Munson, Gorham B., 1926.1; 1928.1
Muir, Edwin, 1955.25; 1957.21
"Museum Gets Work of Marianne Moore," 1970.2
"My Apish Cousins," 1937.3. See also "Monkeys, The"

"N.Y.U. Graduates Warned on Rigid War Attitudes," 1967.5

National Poetry Festival Pro-
   ceedings, 1964.17
"Native American Culture,"
   1956.4
"Native Genius for Disunion,"
   1974.5
Necessary Angel, The, 1951.12
Nemerov, Howard, 1954.21;
   1963.15; 1966.12
"Nevertheless," 1957.25;
   1960.12; 1973.15
Nevertheless, 1944.2-8; 1945.6,
   8-9; 1948.8; 1956.8; 1957.30;
   1970.6
"New Books by Marianne Moore and
   W. H. Auden," 1957.18
"New Books of Poems," 1965.20
"New Books of Poetry," 1941.6
New Era in American Poetry,
   1919.1
"New Euphues, The," 1925.3
"New Poetry," 1968.38
"New Shine on Old Truths,"
   1954.2
"New Slants of Light," 1966.9
"News Notes, 1949.1
"New Verse," 1935.15
"New York," 1975.3
New Yorker profile, 1957.27
Nichols, Lewis, 1954.22; 1957.22;
   1958.12
"Nine Nectarines," 1935.3;
   1951.4; 1957.25; 1971.18
Nitchie, George W., 1969.18, 20;
   1970.1, 17; 1971.4, 11, 13,
   17; 1972.17
Nixon, Richard M., 1972.7
"Nixon Mourns Death of Poet,"
   1972.7
Norman, Charles, 1958.13; 1960.15
Norman, Gertrude, 1961.11
"No Swan So Fine," 1935.9;
   1954.24; 1958.7; 1961.12;
   1966.20
"Note on Her French Aspect, A,"
   1964.21
"Notes," 1957.31
"Notes and Queries," 1964.10
"Notes Etc. on Books Etc.,"
   1965.4; 1968.9

"Notes on Eleven Poets," 1945.4
"Notes on People," 1973.5
"Notes toward a Resemblance:
   Emily Dickinson, Marianne
   Moore," 1964.11
"Nothing Will Cure the Sick Lion
   but to Eat an Ape," 1925.12
"Novices," 1964.23; 1965.8
Nowlan, Alden A., 1960.16
"Number of Things: The Dial
   Award, A," 1927.2
Nyren, Dorothy, 1960.17

Obituaries, 1972.1, 3-5, 7-9, 11,
   18-20
"Obituary Notes," 1972.8
"Oblique Critic," 1956.13
"Observations," 1918.1; 1925.5;
   1935.19
Observations, 1925.1, 4-7, 11,
   15-16, 19; 1929.4; 1931.2;
   1935.3, 13; 1943.2; 1965.10;
   1970.6
Obsessive Images, 1960.4
"Occasionem Cognosce," 1969.25
O'Connel, Margaret F., 1965.16
O'Connor, William Van, 1948.10;
   1962.19
"Octopus, An," 1931.1; 1935.3;
   1937.3; 1962.12; 1963.19;
   1964.40; 1965.14; 1966.6;
   1967.9, 29; 1975.3
O'Doherty, Brian, 1962.20
O'Gorman, Ned, 1955.26
"Old Tiger," 1950.2
Olson, Elder, 1957.23; 1958.14;
   1976.5
"On Being Modern with Distinc-
   tion," 1948.12
"On Mariamna de Maura," 1964.24
"On Reading Marianne Moore,"
   1954.28; 1970.7
On Value Judgments in Literature,
   1976.5
Opening of the Field, The,
   1960.8
Opus Posthumous, 1957.29
Ordinary Universe, The, 1968.21
"Originals and Eccentrics,"
   1929.2

O'Sullivan, Maurice J., Jr.,
    1974.5
"Others," 1918.3; 1919.1
Others, 1918.1-3; 1919.1; 1920.1;
    1921.3; 1946.8; 1953.11
"O to Be a Dragon," 1966.20;
    1969.25; 1971.18
O to Be a Dragon, 1959.2-3, 5-6,
    8-9, 11, 13; 1960.2, 6,
    9-14, 16, 19
"Our Miss Moore," 1962.11
Our Singing Strength, 1929.2
"Ousted Student Booed at
    Harvard," 1969.22
"Outdoor Readings of Poetry
    Started," 1962.1
Owls and Artificers, 1971.5

Paige, Nancy, 1965.17
"Palindromes, Poems, and Geomet-
    ric Form," 1976.6
"Pangolin, The," 1957.25;
    1966.20; 1967.29; 1972.13;
    1973.15; 1975.3
Pangolin and Other Verse, The,
    1936.2, 6; 1970.6
"Pangolin of Poets, The,"
    1941.10
"Paper Nautilus, The," 1964.40;
    1967.29; 1969.25; 1973.15
Paris Review interview, 1961.8-9
Parkin, Rebecca Price, 1966.19-20
"Parnassus Is a Rugged Mountain,"
    1955.22
Parsons, I. M., 1934.2; 1935.15
"Past Is the Present, The,"
    1935.3
Patterson, Floyd, 1962.20
Pavlova, Anna, 1956.9
Payne, Robert, 1964.24
"Peaceable Kingdom of Marianne
    Moore," 1948.8; 1950.1
Pearce, Roy Harvey, 1961.12;
    1970.13; 1971.11
Peltz, Mary Ellis, 1935.16
"People," 1952.11; 1968.10
"People's Surroundings," 1927.3;
    1942.2; 1971.18
Perkins, Ann, 1962.21

Perrault, Charles. See Puss in
    Boots, The Sleeping Beauty,
    & Cinderella
"Personae," 1934.1
"Pertinence of Marianne Moore's
    Notes to 'The Jerboa,'"
    1962.14
"Peter," 1936.1; 1954.24; 1957.25
Petschek, Willa, 1968.33
"Philadelphia Loan," 1973.6
Phillips, James E., 1958.15
"Place for the Genuine, A,"
    1957.28; 1968.36
"Place for the Genuine: The Po-
    etics of Marianne Moore, A,"
    1972.13
"Places, People, Things," 1964.29
Pleasure Dome, 1949.2
Plimpton, George, 1964.25;
    1969.19
"Plumet Basilisk," 1951.4;
    1971.18
Poe, Edgar Allan, 1925.19; 1948.1
"Poems," 1922.1
Poems, 1921.1-3; 1922.1; 1923.5;
    1964.1; 1967.21; 1969.18;
    1970.6
"Poems: Marianne Moore," 1923.2
"Poems for the Eye," 1951.2
"Poems of Fastidious Pattern,"
    1935.14
"Poet as Critic, The," 1955.26;
    1956.5
"Poet for the Brooklyn Dodgers,"
    1968.33
"Poetic Power," 1948.14
"Poetic Theory of Marianne
    Moore," 1975.9
"Poet in the Playpen, The,"
    1964.19
"Poetry," 1932.1; 1935.3, 11;
    1936.3; 1948.7: 1955.17;
    1956.8; 1958.9; 1967.24;
    1968.16, 31, 41; 1969.13,
    24-25; 1972.13; 1975.1, 3,
    4; 1976.7
"Poetry--For Whom?" 1966.16
"Poetry--What Should We Ask of
    It?" 1956.19
Poetry and Fiction, 1963.15

Index

Scott, Winfield Townley, 1952.7; 1957.28; 1961.15
"Sea Unicorns and Land Unicorns," 1925.15-16; 1959.7; 1963.4
Seaver, Edwin, 1925.11
"Secrecy of Marianne Moore, The," 1965.8
"See in the Midst of Fair Leaves," 1953.22
Segnitz, Barbara, 1973.13
Seldes, Gilbert, 1927.2
Selected Criticism: Prose, Poetry, 1955.10
Selected Essays of William Carlos Williams, 1954.30
Selected Fables, 1956.20
"Selected for Poetry Award," 1941.2
Selected Letters of E. E. Cummings," 1969.6
"Selected List of Children's Books, A," 1963.3
Selected Poems, 1935.1, 4-8, 10-22; 1936.1, 3, 5; 1937.1; 1944.4; 1951.11; 1957.30; 1961.12; 1964.9; 1965.7; 1968.41; 1970.6
Selected Poems (1969), 1969.12
Selected Prose, 1909-1965, 1973.12
Sense and Sensibility in Modern Poetry, 1948.10
Sergeant, Howard, 1951.10; 1965.18
"70 Attend Birthday Party for Marianne Moore," 1962.4
"75 Alumnae Receive Bryn Mawr Awards," 1960.3
Seymour-Smith, Martin, 1968.35
Shankar, D. A., 1962.24
"Shaper of Subtle Images," 1972.20
Shapiro, Karl, 1959.11
Sheehan, Ethna, 1963.17
Sheehy, Eugene P., 1958.16-17
"She Has Iron in Her Writing," 1966.17
Sherman, W. D., 1972.17
"She Taught Me to Blush," 1964.2
Shipman, Jerome, 1969.11

Short History of American Poetry, A, 1974.6
Shuster, George N., 1935.18
"Silence," 1935.3, 9; 1957.30; 1964.20; 1967.29; 1968.11
Simmonds, C. H., 1965.19
Simpson, Louis, 1963.18
Sitwell, Edith, 1921.2; 1929.3; 1960.5-7; 1965.11
Six American Poets, 1971.6
Sixty American Poets, 1896-1944, 1954.26
Skelton, Robin, 1964.33
"Sketches of the Pulitzer Prize Winners in Journalism," 1952.13
Smith, A. J. M., 1935.19
Smith, Peter Duval, 1951.11
Smith, William Jay, 1964.33; 1965.20; 1968.36
"Smooth Gnarled Crape Myrtle," 1971.18
Snodgrass, W. D., 1954.24
Snow, Wilbert, 1925.12
"Sojourn in the Whale," 1923.5; 1942.2
"Some American Poets," 1935.7
"Some Characteristics of Marianne Moore's Humor," 1966.20
Sound and Form in Modern Poetry, 1964.12
Southworth, James G., 1954.25
"Speaking of Books," 1952.1
Spender, Stephen, 1956.20
Spenser, Edmund, 1941.12; 1966.18
"Spenser's Ireland," 1942.2; 1957.25; 1966.18; 1974.5
"Sports Department," 1960.9
Sprague, Rosemary, 1969.26; 1970.12
Stallknecht, Newton P., 1973.14
Stanford, Donald E., 1972.18
Stapleton, Laurence, 1958.18
Stauffer, Donald Barlow, 1974.6
"Steeple-Jack, The," 1935.3, 20; 1953.9; 1956.8; 1957.30; 1958.7; 1964.20, 40; 1967.29; 1968.31; 1970.14; 1973.15
Stegner, Wallace, 1973.5
Stein, Gertrude, 1923.2; 1925.3
Steloff, Francis, 1975.10
Stephan, Ruth, 1964.31